# Defi, Bitcoin and Cryptocurrency Trading and Investing

## for Beginners

*Utilizing Decentralized Finance, Binance Trading, Tax Strategies, and Technical Analysis for Lending And Borrowing (2022)*

## Kenneth Vaughn

# Table of Contents

# INTRODUCTION

This book focuses on investing and trading Decentralized Finance protocols, Bitcoin, Ethereum, and altcoins, and offers many tactics and strategies for doing so. First, you'll learn how to reduce your crypto taxes to a bare minimum, allowing you to keep a larger portion of your earnings. Following that, you'll discover how to apply technical analysis for cryptocurrency trading and how to trade cryptocurrencies on Binance. Following that, you will learn how to value any cryptocurrency using tokenomics and which DeFi systems perform the best. Following that, you will discover how to trade bitcoin, bitcoin options, and bitcoin futures. Following that, you will learn how to DYOR (do your own research) on any cryptocurrency and the best practices for avoiding crypto frauds. Finally, you'll discover how to invest in decentralized ICOs as well as how to invest in and trade bitcoin IPOs like a pro. If you're ready to dive in, let's first talk about how to reduce your crypto taxes so that any extra money stays in your pocket.

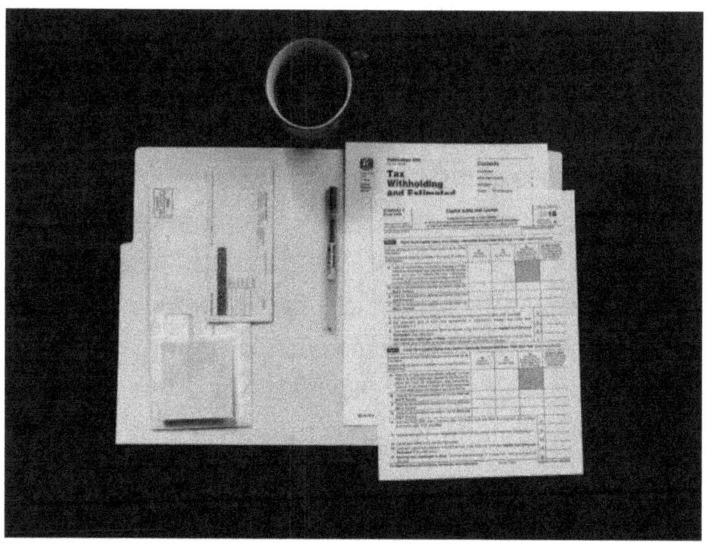

# CHAPTER 1:  HOW TO CUT YOUR CRYPTO TAXES DOWN

Nothing makes governments happier than our hard-earned money. Many of you will most likely be realizing your crypto gains this year, which will have ramifications for your tax bill next year, when you may find yourself getting pleasantly shafted by the taxman. I don't know about you, but I'd rather the money stayed in my pocket than end up in the hands of some corporate officials in government. Fortunately, there are several things you can do to lower your crypto tax burden, as well as many places you may go to pay no taxes on your crypto winnings. If you're serious about maximizing your profits during this bull market, it's time to look at the tax optimization options accessible to you. By the end of this chapter, you'll have all the tools you need to ensure that your Lambo doesn't turn into a Fiat Punto when it's time to sell.

To begin, I'd like to state unequivocally that everything in this chapter is perfectly legal. That's because what I'm going to talk about today isn't tax evasion, but rather tax avoidance. The devil is in the details, and these are the kinds of minutiae that the wealthy and powerful are well-versed in. There are plenty of legal ways to avoid paying taxes, but the truth is that they aren't generally worth it unless you make a lot of money. Setting up a shell business in the Caribbean or temporarily relocating to another country, for example, is pointless if you only stand to save a few thousand dollars in crypto tax. As a result, the first step is to calculate how much money you intend to gain from cryptocurrency in 2021. If it appears that you may make more than a million dollars in cryptocurrency this year, I would strongly advise you to consult with a professional to see what choices are available to you.

If you plan to make less, I have a few crypto tax recommendations for you. My first piece of crypto tax advice is to minimize taxable occurrences to a minimal. What exactly do I mean by this? In most jurisdictions, the only crypto-related transaction that is tax-free is the conversion of fiat to crypto. Almost everything else is a taxable event in the eyes of the tax authorities. Even crypto-to-crypto transactions are sometimes taxable, which can be a major hassle when it comes time to submit your forms. Ideally, you should be storing your cryptocurrency and just adding to your portfolio with Fiat whenever you see fit. The only taxable occurrences should be when you convert your crypto to fiat. This is much easier said than done, and if you're a casual trader like me, you've probably already done a good amount of crypto-to-crypto transactions, received some staking rewards, been airdropped a few odd tokens, and occasionally bought groceries using a crypto debit card. Instead of trying to make sense of it all on your own, you may use crypto tax software to assist you. Crypto tax software is improving by the day.

My second crypto tax advice is to consider if it would be worthwhile to realize some of your gains in the coming calendar year. Whether or not you can do this depends on how the bull market plays out and what coins or tokens you own, but here's how it would work in general. Let us first assume you live in a country with a tax year that corresponds to the calendar year (January to December). Assume it is mid-December 2021. The majority of the cryptocurrencies you invested in have recently surpassed their all-time highs, and you've concluded that now is a good time to cash out. Depending on how much you've gained and the tax plan where you live, it may be preferable to pay out half of your gains right immediately and save the remainder until the first week of January in 2022. This splits the taxable gains across two years, potentially increasing your income even if the price of the cryptocurrency you're holding falls by a few percentage points over that period. If the price of the cryptos you intend to sell rises during that time, all the better. If you live in the United States, use the following link to a tax calculator to figure out whether spreading your gains over two years will save you tax.

<https://www.nerdwallet.com/article/taxes/capital-gains-tax-rates>

Here's an example of a computation you'd need to perform. Assume you paid $100,000 for one Bitcoin. Bitcoin is now worth $100,000 in mid-December 2021. You want to examine if it makes tax sense to realize half of those earnings now and wait until January 2022 to realize the other half. You would enter the whole $100,000 into the tax calculator's sale price box to determine the tax on your capital gain. In this situation, it is approximately $26,000. Then, enter half of that amount to see what the capital gains tax would be in 2021. In this situation, it's about $8,700. Because the capital gains tax will be roughly the same in 2022, dividing your gains across two calendar years will save you a few thousand dollars in taxes. If you decide to quit your job and take a year to discover something you genuinely enjoy doing for a living now that you have some money to sit on, you might potentially save even more on taxes. Again, you'll need to research capital gains taxes in your own country and decide whether splitting up your income between 2021 and 2022 is worthwhile.

Keep in mind that the value of your cryptocurrency may fluctuate during this time. My final crypto tax recommendation is to investigate whether working as a freelancer or creating your own business may help you offset some of your crypto gains. Many of the items purchased by freelancers and businesses can be deducted as business expenditures. These expenses are subtracted from the tax they must pay, which is one of the reasons why some of the world's greatest corporations officially pay no tax. It's simply because their expenses equal or exceed their revenues. Some argue that the capacity to deduct expenses is what distinguishes the middle class from the upper class. As a regular employee, your earnings are taxed twice: once when you earn them and again when you spend them. When you work as a freelancer or own a corporation, on the other hand, practically everything is tax deductible.

If you're going to cash out your crypto, I'm guessing you'll spend some or all of that money on anything, whether it's a car, a house, or stuff linked to one of your interests. As an example, if you've always wanted to buy a fine boat, you could form a corporation, buy a boat, claim it as a business cost, and pay no tax on it. I should point out that this is probably a lot more complicated than I make it out to be, and it might not even be possible where you live. If it turns out to be possible, make sure to do it with the assistance of a tax advisor.

My fourth cryptocurrency tax suggestion is to look for any loopholes in your country's tax legislation. Gift giving is one of the most common tax loopholes. Giving bitcoin as a gift is not a taxable event in some countries, and the person receiving it may be allowed to sell it and pay no capital gains if the value of the crypto in Fiat is the same or less than when they received it. This is an excellent alternative if you intend to spend your crypto profits on something that will be shared with members of your family or someone you trust. Argentina, Australia, Austria, Cyprus, India, New Zealand, Norway, Slovakia, and Sweden are just a few of the countries with no gift tax, and the list is much longer when it comes to gifting cryptocurrencies, as many governments consider cryptocurrency to have no actual value until it is converted into Fiat currency.

If you are a family guy in one of these countries who wants to buy a lovely big car for his wife and maybe children, you could perhaps donate the monies to your wife and have her purchase the car under her name. I do not advocate this if you have even the slightest concern that the individual to whom you intend to gift your cryptocurrency may steal your sats. I will also warn you that gift giving can often be a murky area, especially when it comes to purchasing items that may be returned to you in the future. For example, if you inherit a house that was previously acquired with gifting bitcoin, you may be in danger. If there is one crypto tax scheme for which you should seek professional tax guidance, it is gift giving.

Let's imagine you're dissatisfied with these solutions, or you've discovered that they won't work for you, or you even insist on paying no tax since taxation is theft. If this is the case, your only option is to relocate to a country that does not tax cryptocurrency earnings. Before I list these countries, I'd like to emphasize what I said earlier: you must decide whether it's worth your time and money to relocate. It also goes without saying that you should visit these countries before making your decision. The United Arab Emirates is the preferred tax refuge for crypto moon boys. The UAE has no capital gains or income taxes. It is also quite welcoming to outsiders and is widely regarded as a fully developed country with first-rate services and amenities. There are also plenty of low-cost Lamborghinis on the market. That being said, living in the UAE may be incredibly expensive, and it is extremely hot all year round due to the fact that you are in the middle of the desert. It's worth remembering. It can also be difficult to obtain the visa required to reside in the UAE full-time, so if these are something you can live with, I recommend contacting the nearest UAE Embassy or consulate for further information.

Speaking of difficult-to-obtain citizenship, Switzerland is another crypto tax haven, but only if you believe yourself to be a professional crypto trader. Receiving this designation appears to be difficult, but the result is that all of your gains are taxed at near-zero rates. The negative is that Switzerland has an annual wealth tax that takes into account the value of your crypto holdings, and it is also not an easy country to migrate to unless you live in Europe or have intimate relationships with World Economic Forum technocrats. Other European countries considered crypto tax havens include Germany, which does not tax cryptocurrency gains if held for more than a year and provides residency cards to any Europeans, Americans, or Canadians who relocate there. Portugal does not tax crypto profits or income, although it is more difficult to relocate if you are not a European citizen due to visa limitations. Profits from bitcoin trading and mining will not be taxed in Belarus until 2023, but it is currently not a country where anyone should relocate, in my opinion. Finally, Malta collects no taxes on cryptocurrencies held for more than a year but imposes a minimum yearly tax of 15,000 Euros on any non-Europeans who relocate there.

There are three choices for crypto tax havens in Asia. The first is Singapore, which is unsurprising given that it is one of the continent's most important financial centers. Unless you are actively day trading cryptocurrency, you will not be taxed on any cryptocurrency gains in Singapore. Unfortunately, if you do not have a large salary, it is tough to relocate to Singapore. Malaysia is Asia's second crypto tax haven, as it does not tax crypto gains or transactions. To get one of the visas required to go to Malaysia, you'll need significant cash or a high income, just like in Singapore and the UAE.

Hong Kong is Asia's third crypto tax haven, but who knows how long that will survive considering what's been going on with China. This is due to Act 60, which is designed to entice big brains and large money to migrate to Puerto Rico. If you're reading this book in the first quarter of 2021, you may still have time to acquire your residency in Puerto Rico and avoid paying taxes on your crypto income this year. That, I believe, covers nearly every legal alternative for reducing taxes on incoming crypto earnings. Whatever you chose, it is vital that you keep track of your profits and losses.

I know many of you are already doing this, but when the bull market continues and we start to see currencies pump and dump by hundreds of percentage points on a daily basis, it will become much more difficult to maintain track of your portfolio. This is why I use cryptocurrency tax software every year The law-abiding citizens who decide to file their crypto taxes in these countries are being treated as test subjects with authorities pushing them to provide as much information as possible until they can't bear to fork over anymore. Come to think of it, this seems to be what we're seeing with current cryptocurrency regulations.

# CHAPTER 2:  HOW TO USE TECHNICAL ANALYSIS FOR CRYPTOCURRENCY TRADING

Do you ever feel like you have absolutely no idea what you're doing in the crypto market? Do you find yourself constantly buying the top and selling the dip? If you answered yes to both of those questions then I'm afraid you have all the symptoms of one of cryptocurrency's deadliest diseases; technical analysis deficiency syndrome. If this condition is left untreated it could result in an unprecedented loss of cryptocurrency gains, potentially condemning you to a life as a wage slave. Thankfully a cure does exist and I just so happen to be well versed in the ancient teachings of technical trading, which constitutes this cure.

In this chapter, I will be passing some of these lessons on to you so you can overcome this chronic disease, protect your profits and achieve the financial freedom you seek. The first TA topic I want to tackle is trading time frames. When you're analyzing the price of any given cryptocurrency by drawing chart patterns or using technical indicators, what you see can change significantly depending on the time frame you've selected. Most cryptocurrency exchanges offer over a dozen time frames that range from one month to one minute. Some exchanges like FTX's Serum Decks are hoping to make it possible to trade on time frames that are in the milliseconds.

When I look at the daily chart for Bitcoin with the EMA indicators enabled, it looks like we've fallen below our first two levels of support specifically the seven day EMA and the 25 days EMA. Bitcoin is clearly in a Downward trend which suggests that it's about to crash hard, however, when I switch to the weekly chart we are still sitting above the 25-week EMA and the monthly chart shows that we are away a ways from any of the monthly EMA-s. The monthly timeframe also reveals that Bitcoin is in fact still in a strong uptrend. What this means is that Bitcoin has some strong zones of support if the price were to fall and it seems more likely that it will continue to go up in the long term. While that's certainly good news for swing traders and hodlers', I reckon you are here because you want to do some day trading. Let's say that once again we see that scary Downtrend along with some support at the 30K level. There also seems to be some support at the 29K level, some support at 26K, and a whole bunch of support at 23K. To the upside, we seem to have some resistance at 33K, 35.5K, and just under 38K. Since we've been trading sideways for a few days, it's hard to tell what the price is going to do next

Most cryptocurrency exchanges offer some sort of leveraged trading via their futures markets and usually offer anywhere between 1 to 100x leverage with stablecoin settled contracts; meaning you're trading a stablecoin like USDT instead of actual Bitcoin. If you're wondering how exactly leveraged trading works, here is a simple example. Recall the previous day trading time frames I explained to you. Suppose you're certain that Bitcoin's price is going to drop from 30K to 29K and want to profit from this little correction. what you could do is enter a short position you're using USDT. If you short with 1x leverage then you're just using the USDT you own. You aren't borrowing any money. This means that if you shorted Bitcoin with 1x leverage and 3000 USDT you would make 100 USDT in profit if you close your position when the price of Bitcoin drops from 30K to 29K. Not bad right? Well, if you shorted Bitcoin with 100x leverage, you would make 10,000 USDT from that 1K drop in price, 100x more than that 100 USDT. Here's the scary part; if Bitcoin was to go above 30K by just $40, you would lose your three grand. Why? Because you're trading with 100x leverage and 30 times 100 is 3K. If the exchange doesn't liquidate your position then they would be in the negative because they're the ones lending you the money.

Given that Bitcoin's price can fluctuate by hundreds of dollars a second, you are almost guaranteed to lose your money when trading with more than a few times leverage. This is why traders will set something called a stop loss which would automatically close their short position if Bitcoin's price went over 30K by let's say 3 dollars. That doesn't sound like much but that's a $500 loss on that initial 3K. As you can hopefully tell, leverage trading is extremely risky. It's a point that I wish more people understood. If you plan on doing some leveraged trading, I insist that you better educate yourself. Warnings aside, measured leveraged trading can come in handy when the crypto market is in a free fall and there are safer ways to do leveraged trading than using a futures exchange. In May of 2020, Binance introduced leverage tokens to its spot market exchange. Binance leverage tokens are those up and Down tokens you see when you're searching through trading pairs against USDT for major cryptos on Binance. The amount of leverage you get from these tokens fluctuates between 1.25x and 4x depending on market conditions.

In contrast to leverage trading, you technically cannot be liquidated when you hold finance's leverage tokens. Instead, the value of the leverage token simply rises or falls depending on the type of token it is. Using Aave as an example, let's say that Aaveup, which represents a long position and has gone up by 13 percent in the past 24 hours, whereas Aave has only gone up by 7 percent which is almost a 2x leveraged position. By contrast, the Aave Down has dropped by over 22 percent which corresponds to a leveraged position of roughly 3.5x. If you're wondering why the actual dollar price of Aave up and Aave Down are so different, I recommend you read up about Binance's leverage tokens. The main takeaway here is that Binance leverage tokens allow you to long and short major cryptocurrencies with significantly less risk than leveraged trading.

Now that you know how to maximize your profits using leverage, I reckon it's about time I told you how to detect major moves in the crypto market before they happen. The key to spotting a breakout to the upside or a collapse to the Downside is being familiar with the most common price patterns and indicators. Using Bitcoin's recent price action as an example it's quite obvious that we are in a descending triangle. Descending triangles tend to break to the Downside. How low could the price fall? Well, there are a few critical zones to watch. The first is 20K which is how low we should drop according to the descending triangle pattern. This also just so happens to be the support level provided by the 200-day moving Aaverage. Remember, that there's also support at 26K and 23K so if we do touch Down to 20K, we're going to have two stops on the way down and won't be in total freefall. These are the zones where you could set stop losses on short positions or even accumulate some BTC if you're in it for the long haul.

How do we know when the Downwards trend has actually begun? The secret is trading volume. The selling volume has been decreasing in recent days and this suggests to me that people are not too eager to part ways with their Bitcoin and we probably won't be moving too much lower. However, if I see that this selling volume increases and we close the day significantly below that triangle formation, this would confirm a breakout to the Downside. Even though descending triangles tend to break to the Downside, given that we're in a strong long-term bullish trend on the monthly chart, there is a chance that this descending triangle could break to the upside. To confirm a breakout to the upside on Bitcoin, we would need to see a daily close above the sloping edge of the triangle, which is around 33K with lots of volumes. This conveniently corresponds to the 33K resistance level. In terms of estimating how high we can go, the same rules apply as before. The triangle pattern alone suggests that we could go back to Bitcoin's all-time highs in the low 40K-s. If we do reach that price we are likely to have a couple of stops along the way at 35.5K and 38K. This means that you could go long and set a stop order around those price ranges, or take some fiat profits if that's what you're into.

There's just one last thing to figure out and that's where the next levels of resistance could be when Bitcoin pushes past its previous all-time high of 42K. While price patterns and technical indicators go a long way in day-today trading, it's a whole different ball game when prices start to go parabolic. That's because you're in uncharted territory and the absence of any resistance in front of an upward price trend, means there is no way of knowing what the next high is going to be. Take Theta for example. The price of the token went from about 70 cents in early December 2020 to nearly two and a half dollars in early January 2021. I had a feeling it would see explosive growth because of its absence of any previous resistance as a newer altcoin. I reckon you could have predicted Theta's January top using the Fibonacci indicator which is how many crypto traders guesstimate the next resistance levels for Bitcoin when it pushes past previous all-time highs.

When you're trying to predict how high the price could go using the Fibonacci indicator you draw it using the swing high and the swing low as reference. In this case, the swing high I would be using is Bitcoin's previous all-time high and the swing low is the lowest price Bitcoin has seen in this four year cycle. Based on this, the next area where we could see some resistance is around 46.5K. The next level after that would be around 63K and finally 73K. It's worth pointing out that the strong 30K support we've seen recently is also reflected in the Fibonacci indicator. In fact, it's quite common for prices to bounce between the critical price zones noted by the indicator and I imagine we will see some similar sideways action in the next two zones as well. Besides the Fibonacci indicator, there are also a few key psychological price levels to keep in mind, namely the 100K mark which is where many people are going to take some profits.

The smarter traders in the crowd will probably do something akin to front running. This is where you sell your Bitcoin a few hundred or even a few thousand dollars below a key resistance level. It is a clever tactic but be aware that it doesn't always work and many of these traders realized soon afterwards that they sold way too early. When the time comes, it will be up to you to use your judgment. To my trading strategy, scalp trading is completely out of the question. It's like a vanilla version of leveraged trading and when you mess with leverage I find it's too easy to get carried away and in almost every case. The risk outweighs the reward because you will get wrecked more often than not even with stop losses. If you insist on getting as much profit out of this market as you can, leverage tokens are a great alternative. Spotting a new price trend boils Down to trading volume. It is that crucial piece of context that's often ignored when the price of Bitcoin starts to fall. Whenever you feel the fud coming on taking a moment to exercise that ta muscle and see if there really is cause for concern. Pulling out that Fibonacci indicator from time to time is also a nice way of reminding you of the bigger picture. Cryptocurrency still has a really long way to go as an asset class and even though the road is not straight, I am quite confident that it will become the most valuable market on the planet besides the derivatives market of course.

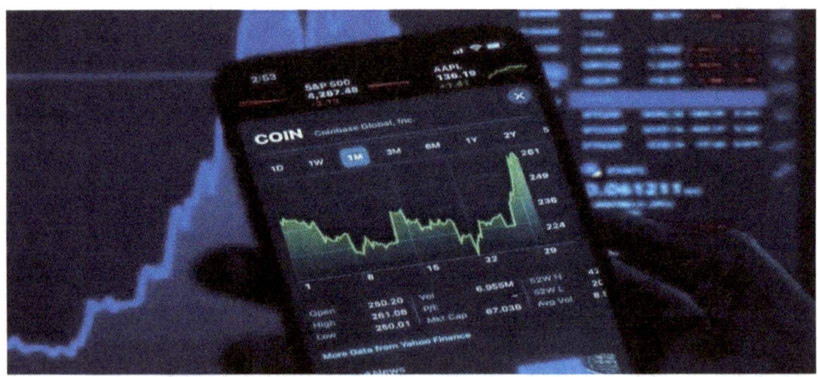

# CHAPTER 3:   HOW TO TRADE CRYPTOCURRENCIES ON BINANCE

Have you discovered a legendary altcoin and need to venture beyond Coinbase to obtain it? If you agree with any of that, you'll probably want an exchange that gives you access to hundreds of altcoins and trading pairs. One that allows you to deposit Dollars, Pounds, Euros, or maybe you want to trade futures, get interested in your crypto, acquire a crypto visa card, or participate in one of those mystery IEOs like the one your friend earned a lot of money in? The good news is that there is an exchange that provides all of this and more. Binance is the world's leading cryptocurrency exchange.

So, in this chapter, I'll show you how to buy Bitcoin with regular fiat currency, how to trade on the exchange and give you a comprehensive overview of Binance's other major features. In fact, the inverse is true. Binance's renowned founder Changpeng Zhao, or CZ, is making waves and taking names in interviews, on Twitter, and even on the cover of Forbes magazine. According to Forbes, CZ is the fifth wealthiest person in cryptocurrency, having a net worth of 1.9 billion dollars. Binance exchange debuted in 2017 following a successful initial coin offering (ICO) that raised $15 million USD. Those investors received BNB coins in exchange for an initial value of about 10 cents. In today's world, BNB is worth more than $100. Not a terrible return for those that believed in CZ from the start.

Binance reported profits of roughly 570 million USD in 2019, with CZ indicating at the end of 2020 that the exchange planned to record profits of around 1 billion USD for the year. Binance processes over 2 billion deals each day on average, which accounts for the insane gains. Binance, however, does not end there. In fact, the exchange has a considerably larger stake in the crypto ecosystem than Binance alone. Last year, it purchased Swipe, a crypto card supplier with a project worth roughly $200 million dollars. Binance also purchased coinmarketcap.com and the famous crypto storage solution

Trust wallet in 2018 for an estimated $400 million USD. Other strategic investments include the FTX exchange, whose token is a top 40 crypto in its own right and has a market worth of about $2 billion USD. Binance also has a track record of doing the right thing. They were hacked in 2019 and approximately 2% of the Bitcoin holdings on the exchange were lost, but Binance fully paid everyone affected by that theft by drawing cash from the Safu fund, which is a pot of cryptocurrency set aside to handle incidents like exchange hacks. Binance is a huge deal in the crypto world, and they have a track record of taking care of its customers.

All of these are significant reasons why I am pleased to use Binance as my primary cryptocurrency exchange. Now that you've seen the outline, I'd like to explain how to find out if the hot altcoin you're looking for is truly listed on the exchange. After all, there's no use in setting up an account if it doesn't exist

However, I'd want to move on and discuss how to deposit fiat currency, specifically dollars and euros, on Binance. After you've set up your Binance account and secured it with a strong password and two-factor authentication, you're ready to get started and make a deposit. The fact that there are so many possibilities makes Binance a wonderful exchange for getting started with cryptocurrency. You'll notice a currency symbol if you click the buy crypto button at the top of the home page. When you click on it, a drop down menu will appear with all of the different fiat currencies you can deposit in. There are literally dozens of different currencies from which to pick. The payment choices will vary depending on the currency you choose. Binance has the widest range of currencies from which to purchase cryptocurrency. What's also amazing about Binance is that some of these deposit options have no fees, so you'll receive the most bang for your cash. If you live in the United Kingdom, you'll probably want to use that no-fee bank deposit to get those Pounds into Binance. Sepa deposits are free if you live in Europe. You can also avoid fees on Australian deposits by utilizing Pay ID or Osco. I should point out that not every country will have fee-free deposit choices, so keep that in mind. Those who are tempted to just use their bank card to make a deposit on Binance should reconsider. Although it is handy, Visa or Mastercard deposits will be levied at 1.8 percent for Euros or GBP and 3.1 percent for Rubles. If you live in one of those countries where the sole choice is to pay exorbitant card costs on Binance, you should consider using a local exchange with cheaper fiat on-ramp fees. You may then send Bitcoin from this exchange to Binance to purchase that trendy altcoin.

Another thing to keep in mind is that, while Binance accepts a wide range of currencies, it does not support every currency in the world. So, if your home currency isn't accepted, you'll probably want to deposit US dollars. When you click Choose a Deposit Method, you will be directed to the deposit page. If you chose a bank deposit, you'll be presented with two options. You can pay the 1.8 percent fee by depositing with a bank card, which is as simple as entering the amount you wish to deposit, clicking continue, entering your card details, and hitting the pay button. You can also make a free bank deposit. In the United Kingdom, you can make use of a service called quicker payments. The only drawback to this choice is that you'll need to submit some more ID information. However, it is as simple as pulling out your passport, entering your passport number, and selecting your nation. After that, you'll see some bank information to utilize to make your deposit. You can just log in to your online banking account and make the transfer.

What's crucial to remember is that you must use the same payment reference that you see in Binance for that transaction. Binance will then recognize that it is your deposit and should be assigned to your account. After your deposit has been processed and you have those Pounds or Euros in your Binance account, return to the buy crypto tab and select cash balance from the drop down menu. You'll then be taken to a screen where you can enter how much and which cryptocurrency you wish to purchase and then click the buy button. You may also view how much cryptocurrency you'll receive before you make the purchase.

If you want to deposit on Binance, that is all there is to it. But what if you already have some crypto and want to join in the exchange's altcoin buffet? To deposit cryptocurrency on Binance, first, log into your account and then click the wallet option at the top left of the screen. This will open a drop down menu where you will see the terms fiat and spot. Simply click on that. You'll next be sent to the screen where you may make your deposit. You'll next be taken to a Bitcoin deposit page with a BTC address. If you wish to deposit BTC, simply use that address to transfer your Bitcoin to Binance. If you want to deposit an altcoin instead, simply click the Bitcoin button to expand a drop down and search for the crypto you want to deposit on Binance. Then you can construct a deposit address to send that cryptocurrency to Binance for trading. You now have a general understanding of how to deposit funds on Binance.

Now I'd like to tell you how you can reduce your trading expenses. I also have some pointers on where to look for Binance promos to take advantage of. Fees may appear to be uninteresting, but trust me when I say that they pile up and can cost you a lot of money in the long run. To begin, you need to be aware that there are two types of cryptocurrency trading costs. The first is the taker fee, which is charged when an order is executed at the current market price. Second, there is something known as a maker charge, which you pay when you offer liquidity by placing things like limit orders. I'm willing to predict that the vast majority of newcomers to cryptocurrency will be paying taker fees, so let's concentrate on that for the time being. The taker and maker fees begin at just 0.1 percent. To put this in perspective, Coinbase Pro charges a fivefold higher default taker cost of 0.5 percent.

There are various ways to decrease your loan expenses even further. The first is to trade more than 50 Bitcoin within 30 days. That's a lot of trade activity. Alternatively, if you have more than 50 BNB in your account, you will receive a significantly reduced maker cost. 50BNB is worth more than 5,000. If you wish to avoid the taker costs, you must trade 4,500 BTC in 30 days or keep 1000 BNB. That's more than $100,000 in BNB coin. Who has that kind of cash lying around? Trying to lower those trading expenses by increasing trading volumes or holding BNB alone is therefore suboptimal. Instead, I keep a little amount of BNB in my account and utilize it to cover my trading fees. If you do this, you will immediately receive a 25% discount on those fees and will pay only 0.075 percent.

Another thing that I notice many people overlooking are Binance's excellent promotions. The majority of these promos are aimed at crypto trading enthusiasts, but it is still worth your time to go through and see if you may benefit from any of them. If you wanted to trade Reef, for example, there was a $50,000 trading competition going on. Despite the fact that the majority of the money goes to the most ardent traders, there is frequently a lottery component to the promotion. In this Reef trading competition, 20 lucky participants who have traded Reef were chosen at random, and each received $500 in Reef tokens. You now understand how to decrease trading fees and take advantage of discounts.

But, since I'm sure you're eager to start trading altcoins on Binance, let's see how it's done. On Binance, you can trade in a variety of methods. Let's start with the simplest option. To begin, ensure that you are logged into your Binance account, then click trade from the top menu bar and pick convert from the drop-down menu. You'll then be brought to a screen where you can choose which cryptos to convert and how much money to swap. You might convert 100 BNB to BUSD. Simply type it and bash preview conversion. You'll see a fee quoted, and you'll have a few seconds to accept it. Your transaction is now complete. It's literally that simple. The disadvantage of this strategy is that it only offers a limited number of trading pairs and only accepts market orders, which means you must accept the current market price. Personally, I prefer greater freedom, which the old trading panel provides. You may go there by selecting trade from the top navigation bar and a classic from the drop down menu. You'll then be taken to a trading screen.Take a deep breath and don't panic if that appears complicated. I assure you that it is not as difficult as it appears. The benefit of using this form of trading interface is that it allows you to place more complicated order types, which can wind up saving you a lot of money and a lot of time.

You most likely have two queries. The first is, what do those 5x and 3x symbols next to some of those trade pairings mean? These just indicate that you can trade on five times or three times leverage through margin trading. This is where you borrow money to trade with leverage and magnify your winnings and losses. If you're just starting out, I strongly advise you to avoid using leverage unless you're an experienced trader who fully understands the hazards. Also, keep in mind that trading pairs employ abbreviated versions of cryptocurrencies known as tickers. This is frequently a three or four letter combination.

But how do you locate the ticker for the cryptocurrency you wish to purchase? You can go to Coinmarketcap and search for the cryptocurrency you're interested in. The ticker will appear to the right of the name of the coin. That method can be used to find the ticker for any cryptocurrency. Returning to the trading panel, market trades may be found in the bottom right corner. This just displays the most recently conducted transactions, and finally, you have the portion of the trading panel where all the magic happens and where you make those all-important orders. This order menu will be set to limit orders by default. An example is the greatest method to explain what these are. So, let's assume I don't like the current Bitcoin pricing, but I'm willing to pay 40,000 dollars for it. I can actually place the order on Binance by entering that 40K price point and selecting the amount of Bitcoin I wish to purchase. If I do that and then create a limit order by hitting the purchase Bitcoin button, the order will be added to the order book. If I'm sleeping and the BTC price on Binance falls to 40K, this limit order should instantly trigger and I'll receive my Bitcoin at this lower price. As a result, limit orders, rather than market orders, may be preferable. It's also worth noting that limit orders incur maker fees rather than taker fees, which can be lower on Binance at times. On the sell side, limit orders function exactly the same way. If the price of Bitcoin exceeds $100,000, I may place a limit order for one Bitcoin. That order will simply sit there doing nothing until the pricing point is met. These orders are, of course, always cancellable. You can optionally specify a time limit for the order to be active.

Market orders are the most basic sort of order. You simply enter the amount you wish to buy and the current market price is used. You should now understand the fundamentals of utilizing market and limit orders to purchase and sell cryptocurrency. One item I'd like to draw your attention to is the futures tab. That's something you should probably avoid. It's riskier than simple margin trading. Professional traders who utilize futures properly can find them to be a helpful tool. However, trading risky altcoins with 125 times leverage is not a responsible usage of them for newcomers. If you insist on trading with leverage, you might want to look into leveraged tokens. These provide moderate leverage while eliminating the possibility of being liquidated, making them a good compromise. That is the fundamental trading functionality on Binance, but it is only one of the many services available in the crypto world.

So, let us see what else is on the menu. With all of this worldwide money printing, I'm sure you're getting low-interest rates on your savings. Binance Earn, on the other hand, allows you to earn interest rates of roughly 6% APY on certain crypto currencies. You have the option of opting for flexible savings, which means you can access your cryptocurrency at any moment. You may also lock in that cryptocurrency for lengths of up to 90 days at a slightly higher interest rate. High-risk savings options with even higher interest rates are available. But keep in mind that you're putting on extra risk in order to achieve that payout. The reason these interest-generating solutions are so popular is that many individuals keep their cryptocurrency in a wallet where it does nothing.

Some people invest a portion of their holdings to generate interest while they wait for cryptocurrency prices to skyrocket to levels they're comfortable with. Binance also has a crypto Visa card, which is a popular offering. What makes you think you'd want one? Let's face it: exchanging cryptocurrency and withdrawing funds from your bank can be a pain. Also, have you ever experienced a 20% rise in a single day? I can tell you firsthand that you'll probably want to go out and treat yourself to something. If this is of interest to you, and you want to be able to spend your cryptocurrency anywhere Visa is accepted, a crypto card is what you need. The good news is that you can get your hands on a beautiful Binance card if you live in most European countries. Binance's black card is absolutely free, and there are no administrative or processing costs. That card also connects to your Binance exchange account, which is very cool. Even better, when you use that card, you can earn up to 8% cashback. So, if you're fortunate enough to be able to obtain a Binance card, you should do so. Although I do not endorse it, Binance also provides collateralized crypto loans.

To put it another way, it's similar to taking a loan from a pawn shop, where you provide collateral in the form of a valuable item, like a watch, and you get cash lent against it. On Binance, you can acquire an initial loan to value ratio of 55%, and if the LTV goes to 75%, you'll be requested to add extra bitcoin to secure your loan. If the LTV reaches 83 percent, Binance will sell your crypto collateral to cover the loan, something you do not want to happen. Most people use these loans to acquire more cryptocurrency, which is a sort of leveraging.

However, if you are interested, you can provide crypto collateral and even be lent Euros, Pounds, or US Dollars. Then there is the Binance Liquid Swap function. That's another option to make passive income with cryptocurrency and potentially earn a big yield but be warned: there are hazards involved.

Then there's something called the Launch Pool. Essentially, this program allows finance users to obtain fresh token incentives in exchange for staking specific cryptocurrencies. Some cryptocurrencies, such as Lit, did not hold a public sale or an initial exchange offering at all, instead of distributing a portion of the initial token through the Launch Pool. The Binance LaunchPad is the final product. This is Binance's exclusive crypto project launch platform. It is also where people may obtain token allocations at extremely low prices. Token allocations for popular Launchpad projects are often done through a lottery system. Simply said, the more BNB coins you have in your Binance account, the more lottery tickets you will receive. If you win the lottery, you will be able to purchase a specified altcoin at a predetermined price. Each winning lottery ticket for the injective public sale on the Binance launchpad entailed the purchase of 200 USD worth of INJ at a rate of 40 cents per token. Within four months, those INJ tokens had risen to about $15 per token. That was a fantastic return for everybody who was involved in it.

If you choose a good project and are lucky enough to secure an allocation, you should do well as soon as public trading on Binance begins. That's why almost every project ever launched on Launchpad has been chronically oversubscribed, and why the lottery system was developed. Binance's endeavor to make these allocations more equitable and fair proved successful. Furthermore, Binance does not share these initial exchange offerings with other exchanges. So, if you see a project on the launch pad, it will be available only through Binance. It's well worth checking over the launch pad to see if anything piques your interest.

Finally, I'd want to take a few moments to discuss some of the free educational tools provided by Binance. The first is Binance Academy, which offers excellent overviews of various cryptos and cryptocurrency-related topics. I would strongly advise you to look into it. Binance research is another area that I believe is neglected. Project reports including a variety of facts and visualizations covering topics such as a project's token supply, token allocation, release timeline, and more can be found here. All of this is provided in an easy-to-digest format. I believe you will find these study papers quite useful in performing your own research. That almost concludes my Binance beginner's guide. To be honest, I've just scratched the surface of what Binance has to offer. There's a lot more, but you should actually start using Binance and discover which choices pique your interest.

# CHAPTER 4: HOW TO VALUE ANY CRYPTOCURRENCY USING TOKENOMICS

Have you ever wondered why cryptocurrencies are so valuable? In a nutshell, they are the only assets that exist outside of the present financial system. They don't require an intermediary to transfer data, most can't be blocked or shut down, and some even provide unprecedented levels of user privacy. The fundamental question is, what makes some cryptocurrencies more valuable than others? Take, for example, Bitcoin and Dogecoin. Dogecoin's programming is based on Bitcoin's coding, and Dogecoin has received nearly as much attention as Bitcoin in recent months. Despite these parallels, one BTC is today worth 60,000 dollars, whereas one Doge is only worth a few cents. Tokenomics is frequently cited as the cause of such a significant disparity in price tags.

Tokenomics are one of the most crucial variables to consider when assessing a cryptocurrency, and it's something that's sometimes missed, so in this chapter, I'll walk you through the many tokenomic factors you should be aware of when vetting a crypto asset. Keeping these in mind will ensure that you make money rather than get rekt'.

Tokenomics is an abbreviation for token economics. Tokenomics encompasses a wide range of variables pertaining to a cryptocurrency coin or token, including supply, allocation, distribution, emission, and utility. It is also crucial to note that, while the terms are frequently used interchangeably, cryptocurrency coins and cryptocurrency tokens are not the same thing. Coins are cryptocurrencies that exist only on their respective blockchains. Consider Cream Finance's Cream token. It is available on Ethereum as an ERC20 token and on the Binance smart chain as a BEP20 token. Tokens are frequently utilized for unique use cases that are peculiar to the projects that created them, rather than for core network activity such as fee payments.

Decentraland's Mana token, which is burned to purchase digital assets on the Decentraland marketplace, is one of the best instances.

The most significant distinction between cryptocurrency coins and cryptocurrency tokens is how authorities treat them. Cryptocurrency coins behave more like currency. This is why the SEC considers Bitcoin and Ethereum to be currencies. The Crypto Ratings Council, a coin-based project, has rated the regulatory risks of most major cryptocurrency coins and tokens on a scale of one to five, with five being the highest risk.

The first tokenomic factor to consider is the currency or token's supply. Some cryptocurrencies, such as Doge, have a large supply, which is why Dogecoin is one of the largest cryptocurrencies by market cap, despite the low dollar value of each coin. This is due to the fact that a cryptocurrency with market size of 1.7 billion is more likely to double in value than a cryptocurrency with a market cap of 8.6 billion. This is why you should always pay attention to a cryptocurrency's market cap rather than the coin or token's actual dollar value, and think in percentage terms rather than dollar terms.

The market cap of each cryptocurrency is derived by multiplying the number of coins or tokens in circulation by the current price of that coin or token. "In circulation" is the essential phrase here. Almost every cryptocurrency has coins or tokens that are no longer in circulation, either because they have been locked or because they have yet to be mined.

A fair launch occurs when a small group of people begins mining a coin or token cooperatively. Fairly launched cryptocurrencies include Bitcoin, Litecoin, and Dogecoin. For fair launch cryptos, there are no coin or token allocations. Allocation is relevant to any pre-mined cryptocurrency. A pre-mine occurs when the project's team mints part or all of the coins or tokens before releasing the network to the public.

A fraction of these pre-mined coins or tokens are typically sold before the network's launch to raise the funding required to create it. As a result, many of today's coins were initially offered as tokens, notably ERC20 tokens on Ethereum. Most pre-mined tokens are often assigned to the team and private investors such as venture capital firms, with only a tiny fraction sold to normal people like you and me in an Initial Coin Offering, or ICO for short.

As a result, many cryptocurrencies have limited circulating supplies. This is an issue because allocating too many coins or tokens to the team and private investors can impede the growth of a cryptocurrency if they start selling their allocations during a bull run. By digging up the ICO specifics for the coin or token you're interested in, you can generally see how these tokens were distributed. Two places where you can readily monitor token allocations are ICO drops and Masari. Be warned that the information on these websites may be inaccurate. If you're looking for a non-Bitcoin coin with its own native blockchain, you'll need to discover its own block explorer. You'll be amazed at how difficult it may be to determine how coins are divided on these block explorers, and I believe this is usually done on purpose to hide how inequitable those distributions are. Using Etherscan as an example, you can see how the decentralized Manner token gets distributed, despite the fact that it was pre-mined.

You might be concerned about those three wallets having a sizable portion of the supply, but if you look closely, you'll discover that they're all smart contracts, not actual wallets. Mana's token distribution is actually fairly good, save from those three smart contracts. There is no single wallet that holds a significant portion of the overall Mana supply. Dogecoin, on the other hand, is not in the same league. Despite the fact that doge is a new cryptocurrency, one wallet has more than 28 percent of its supply. Because there are too many tokens in too few wallets, there is a possibility that these whales will dump their crypto on the market and crash the price at any time. The issue is that what you see on these blockchain explorers is just half the story, due to two additional tokenomic elements.

Vesting and inflation are the fourth and fifth tokenomic elements to keep an eye out for. Vesting refers to how coins or tokens are projected to be allocated in the coming months or years for pre-mined cryptocurrencies. It is usual for pre-mined cryptocurrency projects to lock up a portion of their tokens and gradually release them over time. This gives normal token holders more confidence that the market will not be overwhelmed with tokens allocated to the team and private investors. These vesting schedules are usually rather rational and take place over a long period of time. Unlocking too many tokens at once or in a short period of time can lead to a drop in the price of that token in the short term. A cryptocurrency is either inflationary or deflationary in terms of inflation. Inflation of a cryptocurrency can diminish the value of coins or tokens already in circulation over time. Unless the inflation timetable is exceptionally aggressive, it will have little to no effect on a cryptocurrency's short-term price potential.

Proof-of-stake cryptocurrencies frequently use inflation to reward validators and delegators on their networks. This typically ranges between five and fifteen percent, with some cryptocurrencies, such as Polkadot, altering their inflation dependent on staking participation to preserve network security. Inflation is also used by many DeFi currencies to compensate liquidity providers and Yield farmers on their own networks. DeFi tokens frequently use extremely aggressive inflation schedules to maintain high yearly percentage yields, so much so that Vitalik Buterin compares their tokenomics to the FED's money printer. This is why many people, including Yearn finance founder Andre Cronier, suggest "do not purchase it, earn it," implying that it is preferable to earn these DeFi tokens as a liquidity provider or Yield farmer rather than buy them on an exchange. If a coin is deflationary, a decrease in supply raises the value of that cryptocurrency over time. While this may not have a significant impact in the short term, deflation is one of the reasons cryptocurrencies such as Bitcoin are so valued. Despite the fact that new BTC are mined every 10 minutes, Bitcoin has a maximum supply of 21 million and the quantity of new BTC issued every block is cut in half about every four years. You may believe that Bitcoin has a finite supply that is not deflationary.

The reason Bitcoin is deflationary is due to unintentional loss. Ripple's form a CTO who can't remember the password of a hard drive storing over 7000 BTC is an excellent example of this. Because of human mistakes, these types of incidents will continue, and each time they occur, the overall supply of BTC in circulation decreases. In practice, cryptocurrencies with a limited supply, such as Bitcoin, are deflationary. Some cryptocurrencies, on the other hand, purposefully reduce their supply by burning coins or tokens.

Unfortunately for those who have staked their Eth on Ethereum 2.0, those benefits are unlikely to be realized even if they do occur. This gets me to the final two tokonomic aspects to consider, which are staking and usefulness. When you stake a cryptocurrency as a validator or a delegator, the coins or tokens are often locked up for a period of time. In the event of Ethereum 2.0, any Eth state will not be unlocked until at least 2022. This means that if the price of Eth begins to surge, all of the Eth staked will not make it onto any exchanges. This handily reduces the real circulating quantity of Eth, which may amplify the bullish price action. This effect is significantly stronger for other proof-of-stake cryptocurrencies, such as Polkadot, where more than 60% of the Dot supply is staked. These Dot tokens have a 28-day unlock period. This may not seem like much, but consider that price surges only last a few days or weeks before correcting.

People who are not staking would have more than enough time to take advantage of the lovely bullish price action in 28 days. However, some proof-of-stake cryptocurrencies, such as Cardano, do not have lock-up periods for staked coins. This means that all of that ADA might be traded on exchanges at any time, pushing a parabolic surge back down as people take profits. Staking is a typical benefit for many coins and tokens, in addition to its supply-restricting effects. Utility, often known as a use case, refers to anything that drives demand for a bitcoin coin or token. Bitcoin's principal utility, like gold, is as a store of value. The distinction is that Bitcoin is available to anyone with an internet connection, whereas gold requires a bit more infrastructure to obtain and store.

Given how badly fiat currencies keep their value these days, there is a high demand for a simple store of value like Bitcoin, which is why it is the most valued cryptocurrency on the market. The major utility of Ethereum is to pay fees to use the decentralized applications built on it and to transfer any ERC20 tokens. There are hundreds of DAPps and thousands of ERC20 tokens, which means there is a lot of demand for Eth to pay gas costs, which is why it is the market's second most valued coin. Many DeFi tokens can be used to cast votes in the protocol's governance structure. As a protocol's total value increases, so does the demand for its governance token. Surprisingly, the market capitalizations of several DeFi tokens, such as AAve, are nearly one-to-one with the entire value locked on their systems. This makes it simple to identify DeFi cryptocurrencies that are under or overvalued. There is, however, a new DeFi economy overflowing with these undervalued coins. That's all the tokenomic components you'll need to enter the crypto market.

Cryptocurrency coins and cryptocurrency tokens each have their own set of advantages and disadvantages. While bitcoin tokens may be more profitable investments, they are also riskier to hold due to regulatory risks. Furthermore, token earnings are frequently fleeting, as many cryptocurrency projects employing tokens aren't designed to last more than a few years. Dap cryptocurrency tokens are frequently supported by cryptocurrency coins as part of broader ecosystems. This extends the life of coins and results in a more steady gain in value as their ecosystems develop. This increase in value isn't always clear if you only look at the price. Small circulating supplies may also pose a danger to that value in the near or far future if any of those idle coins or tokens begin to circulate. As a result, I normally evaluate cryptocurrencies based on their completely diluted market capitalizations. This makes it simple to determine if a cryptocurrency is overpriced or undervalued, regardless of its price. Unfortunately, truly valuable fair launch cryptos are becoming increasingly difficult to find these days. While I am not a fan of inflation, I believe that some coin or token printing is required to motivate miners to continue supporting the network.

# CHAPTER 5: WHAT ARE THE BEST PERFORMING DEFI CRYPTOCURRENCIES

Over the course of 2020, the number of DeFi subscribers will have increased from just over 100,000 to well over 1.3 million. This surge in popularity shows no signs of abating, putting pressure on the Ethereum community to come up with solutions to cut gas prices and enhance network efficiency until Ethereum 2.0 is ready to roll. Layer 2 blockchains, for example, enable Ethereum to scale from 15 transactions per second to tens of thousands of transactions per second with near-zero network fees. As a result, demand for layer twos is higher than ever, and the tokens that enable these scaling solutions are primed to experience significant increases in the coming months.

The Matic network is now the leader in the layer 2 space, and by the end of this chapter, you will understand why the Matic token might be one of the top-performing cryptos in 2021. Matic network has a fascinating past. Anurag Arjun, Sandeep Nailwal, and Jaynti Kanani are the project's three co-founders. All three were successful coders and active members of India's Bitcoin community, which was modest given the country's heavy-handed approach to cryptocurrency. Sandeep noted in an interview that India's aversion to cryptocurrencies stems from the country's black market economy, which is reportedly so enormous that if it were factored into GDP, it would place India among the top three largest economies in the world. This makes working in cryptocurrencies a particularly unappealing career choice for most engineers in India, especially after India's central bank prohibited crypto firms from receiving banking services in 2018. However, this did not deter the Matic team, which has been working on a scaling solution for Ethereum since the fall of 2017. The trio was inspired by a technical paper released by Ethereum co-founder Vitalik Buterin and developer Joseph Poon outlining a scaling solution called Plasma. In the year that followed, Matic co-founder Gianti Kanani collaborated with decentraland developers to create More Viable Plasma, a more efficient version of Plasma. Something that is seen as a significant milestone in the Ethereum space. As a result, More Viable Plasma became the foundation for Matic's own technology.

Throughout 2018 and 2019, the Matic team organized and attended dozens of hackathons and cryptocurrency events throughout the world in an effort to raise awareness of the project. Binance approached the Matic team at one of these meetings and offered to fund the project through the Binance launch pad in early 2019. The Matic team accepted, and the token sale took place at the end of April 2019 on Binance. The main net of the Matic network became active in May 2020. This came shortly after the Indian Supreme Court overturned the central bank's cryptocurrency banking ban. As you might expect, the Matic network has grown rapidly since then, and it appears that Matic is quickly becoming the layer 2 solutions of choice for many Ethereum-based projects. This is all due to Matic's unique approach to the Plasma scaling solution, as well as the other beneficial solutions developed by the Matic team for decentralized apps on Ethereum.

To understand how the Matic network works, we must first review Plasma. Plasma entails building a ChildChain, which is simply a clone of the Ethereum blockchain. According to Joseph Poon, Plasma chains are analogous to inferior courts in a judicial system, with the Ethereum blockchain serving as the supreme court. Matic network expands on this concept by including proof of stake in its Plasma chain design. Technically, the Matic network uses the more viable Plasma or MVP. In a nutshell, MVP protects any assets in the Plasma chain by utilizing the Ethereum blockchain.

Despite the fact that the Matic network we see today is linked to Ethereum, the Matic network is blockchain agnostic. That is, it can use any coin blockchain as its foundation layer. Having said that, the Matic network is made up of three levels. The first is an Ethereum blockchain-based smart contract layer. These smart contracts connect the Matic network to Ethereum and include smart contracts for staking, delegation, and any decentralized applications running on the Matic blockchain. The second layer of the Matic network is known as Heimdall, and it is here that validators perform their magic. Bore is the Plasma component of the Matic network. It's where Ethereum developers may re-launch their smart contracts and DAPps. While the Heimdall layer of the Matic network is designed to contain 100 to 120 validator nodes, the Bore layout has a small number of block producers. This is to maintain a one-second block generation time and a breakneck transaction speed of seven to ten thousand transactions per second.

Please keep in mind that this is for a single Matic network side chain. Matic can scale to millions of transactions per second with additional side chains. In terms of fees, one million transactions on the Matic network cost around a dollar. Matic, in addition to its unique architecture, provides two solutions that improve the experience of Ethereum dap users. The first product, Dagger, is characterized as a simple programming tool for obtaining blocks, transactions, or events generated by the Ethereum blockchain. Dagger is essentially a real-world smart contract that performs a function such as sending an email or a phone notice when anything happens on the Ethereum blockchain. For example, you could instruct Dagger to notify you via Telegram if a whale transfers a huge amount of some esoteric ERC20 token to Uniswap. The possibilities are literally limitless.

The Matic wallet, the second product, is intended to serve as a simple gateway to decentralized applications on Matic and Ethereum. Unfortunately, these wallet capabilities do not appear to be accessible yet, and Matic just stated that the mobile version of the Matic wallet would be discontinued. On the Matic network, the Matic wallet is also utilized for staking and delegating. On the Matic network, staking payouts range from 6.5 percent to 650 percent every year, depending on the number of Matic tokens staked. Matic staking rewards are currently well around 30% each year. The hardware requirements for being a validator on the Matic network are likewise fairly reasonable, with only one Matic token required to get started. The stumbling block appears to be the technical knowledge required to get your validator node up and operating. If you're allergic to coding, you can simply delegate. The Matic network web wallet is used for delegation. Staking rewards as a delegator is slightly lower because you must pay your validator dues.

Fortunately, the minimum bet is also one Matic token. To engage with the Matic web wallet, you will need a browser wallet such as Metamask. This implies you'll also require some Eth for gas. Finally, keep in mind that every Matic staked as a validator or delegator has a nine-day unlock period. So, if the Matic token begins to skyrocket, think carefully before locking up your funds. In terms of price activity, does Matic have any real potential? To answer that question, we must first go back in time. Matic Network used the Binance launchpad to launch its debut exchange offering on Binance. 1.9 billion Matic were sold for a total price of $5 million, or slightly more than a quarter of a cent each Matic. Matic network also had two private investment rounds at the end of April, in addition to the IEO. The initial private auction raised $160,000 in return for slightly more than 200 million Matic tokens.

I can't say for certain, but I believe these tokens went to Coinbase Ventures, who invested in the project around that time. Whoever these seed investors were, they got a good deal because each Matic token cost less than a tenth of a penny. The second private sale raised $450,000. This resulted in the sale of 170 million Matics at the same price as the IEO. Only over 23% of Matic's total supply of 10 billion was sold through private sales and IEO. The Matic team received 16 or 1.6 billion tokens from the remaining 77 percent, while advisers from Decentraland and Coinbase received 4 percent. 12 percent of the token supply was set aside for network operations, with the remaining 22 percent and 23 percent going to the Matic foundation and ecosystem incentives, respectively. These coins are subject to a vesting schedule that will run for the next five years, however, I will warn you that the emission timelines you see on Massari and Binance research are not totally right. This is due to the fact that Matic tokens allotted to the Matic foundation and team and unlocked between October 2019 and April 2020 were rerouted to staking rewards. Unlike other proof-of-stake cryptocurrencies, the Matic network does not use inflation to pay validators and delegates, and there are no block rewards. The Matic token has a maximum supply of 10 billion, and the company hopes that by the time their staking rewards run out, there will be enough network activity to compensate validators solely through network fees, which are paid in Matic tokens.

In order to address the question, does the Matic token have a price potential? In terms of tokenomics, things aren't looking bright. Consider that the total number of Matic tokens in circulation has risen from 4 billion to over 7 billion in the last year. Even if Matic has a maximum supply, this does not mean much in practice because a billion tokens are made market ready every six months. It doesn't help that the Matic team was accused of price manipulation after its token plummeted in December 2019. The crash was so severe that practically every major bitcoin news site covered it. It grew so severe that Binance CEO Chen Peng Zhao intervened to dispel the perception that the Matic team was involved in what seemed to be a pump and dump. CZ has a point, and I tend to agree with him. I don't believe the Matic team was to blame for the price movement. They've been extremely open about where their tokens are held and how they've spent on their website. Furthermore, my opinions from viewing interviews with its founders give me the notion that they are not to blame.

Still, I believe there is some form of price manipulation going on with Matic. I've counted at least five pump and dump cycles since the token's debut, though they appear to be becoming less severe each time. This could be due to less speculation and greater interaction on the side of Matic token holders as the Matic network gains traction. Matic Network is collaborating with Decentraland to increase user transactions in its virtual world, and it has also teamed with Maker DAO to bring the Matic network to DIA. Matic announced in September 2020 that it has joined with Circle to issue their USDC stablecoin on Matic. Circle CEO Jeremy Alaire recently tweeted about the Matic network, praising the nearly 33 million USDC in circulation on its network. Awarded that banks in the United States have just been given permission to use stable currencies as part of their operations, some are wondering if Matic will be the Eth layer 2 solution chosen for those stable coin settlements. I believe these institutions will completely diversify their base networks. There is a compelling rationale for them to use Stellar as an example.

Aavegotchi is currently available on the Matic network. What's the big deal about it? Aave founder Stani Kolechov has stated on many occasions that the protocol is being considered for expansion to other blockchains. If the Matic network was not previously on their radar, it most surely is now. Matic co-founder Sandeep Nailwal stated in an interview that they are in talks with huge institutions to supply blockchain services, in addition to relationships inside the crypto field. Sandeep added that this is due to the fact that most private enterprises are aware that blockchains established by companies such as Facebook, IBM, and Google are nothing more than glorified databases.

To top it all off, Matic network was the first to market in its own nation. I can't think of another cryptocurrency project located in India, and I believe it's an area that is frequently disregarded by crypto marketing attempts. When retail FOMO begins to take hold in the coming months, a sizable portion of Indian investors will bet on Matic.

Matic network's interoperability is also a big asset. Other smart contract blockchains like Cardano and Polkadot will soon be establishing their ecosystems and I have a feeling that Matic will play a role on those blockchains as well.

My only significant issue with Matic's design is that it seems to be very concentrated. The actual Plasma chain element of its design is only run by a couple of nodes that probably belong to Matic. If this is the truth and all these block creating nodes are also located in India, any substantial anti-crypto regulation from the Indian government may damage Matic's network. I also question whether Matic network will get enough acceptance to become a sustainable blockchain without the ongoing input of staking rewards. I genuinely do think we will start to see some significant DeFi action on Matic. At the end of the day, that's where the future is and the future is what Matic has been building since its beginnings in 2017. Assuming India doesn't ban crypto trading again, I would not be surprised if Matic becomes one of the most traded cryptos in that country. This combined with user adoption is why I think Matic will likely be the leading layer 2 crypto in 2021.

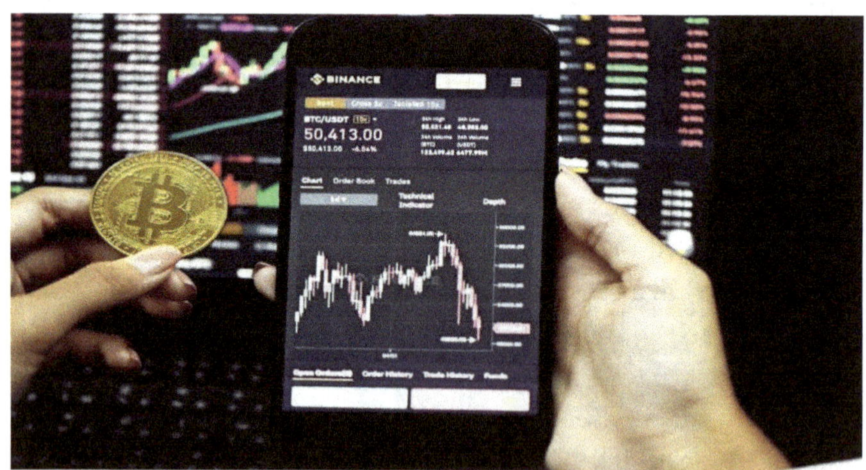

# CHAPTER 6:   HOW TO TRADE BITCOIN OPTIONS

We are all in search of that hidden edge on the markets - that sliver of information that when used appropriately can give us outsized gains over the rest of the crowd. The only problem is that most of this information is reserved for a chosen few. Either that or it's ridiculously expensive to attain, but what if I told you there was a cheap and effective way to get hold of this. A free resource to better read the Bitcoin markets and be two steps ahead. Well, in this chapter I'm going to explain how you can use the Bitcoin options market to your advantage. Not only when it comes to option analysis, but also when trying to determine Bitcoin's price direction. All that is to help equip you with the tools you need to get the market edge.

First I want to start with a quick beginner's overview of options. Quite simply an option is a financial instrument that gives the holder the right to buy or sell an asset at a pre-specified time and at a pre-specified price. All you need to understand are the main drivers of an options price. The first thing that I want to introduce you to is the moneyness of the option. This refers to whether an option is in the money or out of the money. Basically, if you're looking at a call option if the spot price; "S" is above the strike price "K", then the option is in the money. Conversely, if the spot is below the strike it is out of the money. When you have the strike equal to the spot then it is at the money. For a put option, you just flip the arguments for the in or out of the money levels. The moneyness of an option is important as it impacts on the delta variable in the black skulls. Delta is a measure of how sensitive the price of the option is to a change in the price of the underlying asset.

Then you have other factors such as the implied volatility. This is also a very important input in an option price and generally the higher the implied volatility, the higher the price of the option. It's only logical - a more volatile asset will demand a higher option price to make up for the risk in the said asset.

What I really want to explore in this chapter is how to use the option data to infer market trends and sentiment. Firstly I want to discuss the put call ratio. This is a measure of the ratio of the open interest or the volume of the puts versus the calls. The open interest is a measure of the total amount of notional outstanding on a futures or options position, and the volume is of course the total amount of options or futures that have been traded in a certain period.

What can we read from a put call ratio? Well, it's able to give us a rough idea of general sentiment in the market. If there is more open interest outstanding for puts than calls, then that means there are larger bearish bets than bullish bets, hence a put call ratio of greater than one is viewed as more bearish than a ratio of less than one and vice versa. You can also view the put call ratio through time to get a feeling for how this broader market sentiment has changed. You can see the put call ratio over on skew.com. Based on a put call ratio of 1.36, it means that the put option open interest is about 36 percent more than the corresponding call notional outstanding. So, on balance option market participants have more puts outstanding than they do calls.

You may be wondering; why is this relevant? Well, knowing how options traders are positioning themselves, can give you a rough idea of which way they expect the spot market to go, and you should not really be fixated on the absolute number of the put call ratio but rather on how it moves. Whether it's increasing or decreasing, this can help give you a better sense of how that sentiment is changing. That's the put call ratio. Here is the equation that's used to calculate the option 25 delta skew. As you can see, we're trying to get a measure of how much more implied volatility there is on the puts than the calls, relative to a standard measure of the implied volatility. Given the direct relationship between implied volatility and option premiums, you can also view this ratio as a rough measure of how much more the cost of puts are to calls. If we have two options with a similar sensitivity to the price of the underlying asset, how much more are people willing to pay to take on the puts bearish, versus to take on the bullish view with calls.

Let's take a look at a quick example. Let's say that the 25 delta options skew is sitting at about 20 percent. This basically means that the implied volatility of a put option is about 20 percent greater than that of a call. We can also, therefore, infer that the price of similar put options is greater than the calls to a similar degree. This is helpful as it allows you to get a sense of how the relative value and hence sentiment has changed recently. I should also point out that option skew is much broader than just this. You can compare the skew across the entire volatility term structure. You have something called the volatility smile which illustrates this well.

All you need to know about option skew is that it's a helpful metric that you can often use in order to gauge the relative value and sentiment of an option. That's the skew. Now let's move on and take a look at another metric. How cool would it be if you could use the option price to calculate the probability of Bitcoin being above a certain price at maturity? Well, that's actually a reality thanks to the model of the black skull that I mentioned earlier.

If you did stats at Uni, you'll know all about probability density functions like the normal distribution. If it's foreign to you, don't worry. All that we're doing here is using the market parameters of the options in order to back out the probability of it being above a chosen strike price. This is also something that you don't have to calculate yourself.

We can also take a look at the longer term options like the March and June 2021 ones to draw similar probabilities. What can these probabilities tell you? Well, they can give you a rough idea of how likely certain future prices are based on pricing in the options market. The prices that they are willing to pay for option protection and exposure are likely to be a better benchmark for their real price predictions than what they claim on TV.

Of course, I should also caveat that you should not use this as any sort of bible. It's just a probability measure backed out from market data. It's a useful data point you can use in order to further inform your analysis. If there are a lot of options that are expiring on the date, then this could be an indication that there's likely to be quite a lot of volatility on the day.

So the important question here is why and how can you judge the likely price direction on the expiry date? Let's start with that first one. There is volatility around these expiry dates because market participants are trying to adjust their positions for the physical delivery of the underlying asset. Similarly, some market makers May need to adjust their hedge positions in the spot market as they approach these pivotal moments in the option price.

So what you have is a situation in which option expiry events are having a direct impact on the underlying spot markets. When there's a large number of outstanding options, the impact on the spot market is likely to be that much greater. This is something that's been known in the equity markets for a number of years. These are sometimes termed the expiry weeks, where volatility in the underlying share starts to pick up, but given the growth of Bitcoin options, we've also seen these instruments impacting the Bitcoin spot price. This usually tends to happen about two days before the actual expiry. Those participants that hold the option may either close out of their position or roll forward into new options on the expiry date.

So we know that options expiry dates are usually dates of interest when it comes to price movements, but is there a way to get a sense of which way it's likely to move? Well, there's no hard and fast way but you can get a vague idea by taking a deeper look into the options order books themselves. In this case, I'm going to be taking a look at the Deribit order books. They are the exchange with the most liquidity and functionality for retail traders. What we're looking for is to determine how much theoretical buying or selling pressure is likely to come in the spot market from the expiry from these calls or puts in the options market. Basically, to get a rough back of the envelope put call ratio. You want to try and determine the total outstanding notional or open interest on the call and then the put side. With these option expirations, the total open interest on the calls is about 4,200 Bitcoin whereas on the put side the total notional outstanding is about 1,770 Bitcoin. What this tells us is that as we roll forward towards the expiry date, there are a lot more call positions in the market - almost 2.4 percent times more. So, theoretically, this means that there is more chance of there being buying pressure in the spot market as we head into the expiry than selling pressure - a more bullishly positioned market.

Now I should caveat that at the time of doing any analysis if you still have about two weeks to expiry, a lot can change closer to the expiry date and in the Bitcoin markets the impact on spot markets of the open expiry only tends to be felt two or three days before. So if you're going to be using this analysis method, I would encourage you to re-examine the relative open interest balance as we get closer to the expiry time. You should also note that this is not a science. There are many other factors that can swing the price on expiry. Let's not forget that you also have the impact of the futures markets as well as large whale orders going through on the spot market. But it is a handy guide that you can use from time to time. In summary, the truth is that most people who trade options don't really focus too much on the underlying equations. They're more concerned about overarching concepts. Knowing exactly how the 25 delta skew is calculated is of way lesser importance than understanding what it means. What does it show about how the market is positioned and how you can use that information in your broader research toolbox.

Similarly, having a rough idea of what price distributions are in the future, can help you adjust your expectations. Why listen to the moonshot calls of some crypto celeb when you can get a rough idea of price probabilities from the options markets, and it always helps to keep an eye on option expiry dates. Even if you don't try to infer a particular price direction, it has been shown these dates cause spot market volatility. By having these dates pinned in your calendar, you're better prepared to deal with any potential volatility that could result. There's nothing worse than being caught off guard by a large price gap - be it up or down. Therefore I hope you find some of these indicators and tools helpful in your price analysis. They can be that much more interesting when actually used to trade options themselves.

# CHAPTER 7:  HOW TO DYOR (DO YOUR OWN RESEARCH) ON ANY CRYPTOCURRENCY

When it comes to cryptocurrency, there is arguably nothing more important than doing your own research. This is easier said than done. Who has the time to really do their due diligence with any given crypto project? After all, there is a lot of information out there and it can be hard to figure out what's real, what's fake. However, if you're serious about your cryptocurrency aspirations, you are going to need to learn how to do your own research. Research will help you figure out which cryptocurrencies to buy and which ones to stay away from. It will make it easier to figure out when to buy and when to sell those cryptocurrencies and it will even help you educate your friends and family about this magic internet money. If you do enough research, you might even find yourself working full time in the cryptocurrency space so in this chapter I'm going to teach you the art of doing your own cryptocurrency research. I will also reveal the research strategy I personally use.

The crypto market never sleeps and this means that sometimes you can't be waiting for someone else to cover your favorite cryptocurrencies, and now that we're at the start of a bull market, I know that you're all going to have a lot of questions about a lot of different cryptos that I won't be able to answer. This leaves me with one option and that's to teach you the ways of doing your own research. The first step in doing your own cryptocurrency research is figuring out whether the crypto you're interested in is economically active. I can't tell you the number of times that I've come across a promising cryptocurrency project only to check its market activity and see that the coin has been dead for months, or even years. As such, when you hear about a promising cryptocurrency that peaks your interest, the first thing you need to do is go to a website like Coin Market Cap or Coin Gecko to see if it's alive.

In most cases, Coin Market Cap and Coin Gecko will be how you find out about that cryptocurrency, to begin with. If this is the case, be sure to check the training volume and price action you're seeing is genuine. Not only should that token be listed on at least one reputable exchange, the trading volume on that exchange should also be significant. If it isn't, you could find yourself paying a premium, since the order books may not be as deep. If the crypto you're looking at is an ERC20 token that's being traded almost exclusively on a DEXs like Uniswap, be sure to proceed with caution as DEXs do not exactly have any listing criteria or requirements.

This certainly does not write off a project but it is something to keep in mind going forward. That's why you should also pay a visit to Messari, Binance Research, and an ICO tracking site like ICO Drops. When you use these resources, be sure to take notes and write down any questions you might have. You aren't trying to get answers yet. You're just trying to get a primer. In this case, however, what you're looking for on Messari is the profile section of the cryptocurrency you're interested in.

Here you'll often find a thoroughly comprehensive breakdown, including the history of the cryptocurrency, incredibly detailed tokenomics and token allocations, and even a timeline of the project's past and future development and funding milestones. Be sure to jot down the names of any key individuals involved in the project, namely the founder and CEO, assuming they're not the same person - you're going to need this later.

In other words, they basically have to do a good job and get everything right or else fans of the cryptocurrencies they're writing about will launch an attack and they could even see some more severe retaliation from the crypto project itself. The only issue is that the information on Messari and Binance Research is usually a bit outdated. You can't really blame them, considering writing hot off the press crypto content isn't exactly their main shtick. This is why you shouldn't take anything written by a third party as the be-all and end-all of your research, even if that source is reputable. ICO tracking sites like ICO Drops are sort of like time machines in that they often source old images and documentation that's no longer available on the website of the cryptocurrency you're investigating

As such, you should always check and see if they provided any images that can give you a better breakdown of how money was raised and where tokens were allocated. Remember, that Messari does a good job of tracking this so you can compare and contrast Messari's data with what's on ICO Drops to clarify exactly how a given crypto project raised its capital.. This is not a deal breaker but it could be if you see a dead end market when checking a cryptocurrency's tokenomics on Messari.

Assuming that everything seems to look good on that front, it's time to head back to YouTube. Now that you have a good grasp of the new cryptocurrency you're interested in, you'll need to hear it all from the horse's mouth. Moreover, these interviews often go a long way towards helping me wrap my head around any technical elements of a project that I could struggle to understand by just reading their documentation. Watch these interviews on two times speed to save time and take advantage of timestamps if there are any. Chances are the things you hear during these interviews will answer most of the questions you might have had about the cryptocurrency when you read about it on Messari and Binance Research. Watching the brains behind a project in action will also give you a sense of whether you're dealing with the next best thing or with fool's gold.

Also, check the Linkedin profiles to see if their credentials have any merit. This leaves two more steps to your research and that's to fact check everything you've learned so far and figuring out what's in store for this crypto. How many times have you gone to the website of a cryptocurrency you're researching only to feel overwhelmed by the information being offered. I reckon it's a big part of why most people just read the home page and the about section and call it a day.

Unfortunately, most of the information on a given cryptocurrencies website tends to be platitude upon platitude about banking the unbanked or some other noble cause they claim to champion. But since you remembered to write down the key components of how this crypto works, and any questions you might have about it, your next mission is to go through and check that everything you learned still applies and solve any mysteries that might have arisen since you started your research.

Most of this can easily be done by digging through the cryptocurrency's dedicated documentation. If you're lucky, you'll have a friendly search bar where you can just throw in key terms like tokenomics, inflation, ICO, consensus mechanisms, mining, staking, and any other topics that you feel you still need clarification on. Otherwise, you'll have to search through the documents manually. Since cryptocurrency documentation is usually geared towards developers, many of the pages you pull out will contain some lines of computer code. This might seem intimidating but more often than not you'll find that a simple explanation of what's going on is put at or near the beginning of the page in layman's terms. If you're still having trouble finding answers about tokenomics, try and dig up the white paper, find the tokenomics section and see if this provides any additional insight. If it doesn't, try and find a blockchain explorer for that cryptocurrency. If it's an ERC20 token, I recommend using Etherscan.

Here you can quickly check who the largest token holders are, and you can even see the token distribution in a pie chart. Be on the lookout for any wallets that are holding a substantial amount of the token and remember that the largest wallets you see will sometimes be smart contracts used for things like staking. If your cryptocurrency of choice isn't an ERC20 token, hopefully, the blockchain explorer for it will also let you see the rich list of token holders. If not, consider that a red flag. After you've ironed out any flaws in your comprehension of the cryptocurrency, the final thing you should do is check to see whether there are any crucial improvements to the project that are on the way or have already occurred. For the final stage of your cryptocurrency investigation, you'll need three things: a roadmap, a blog, and news, in that sequence, because what you find in the news about a cryptocurrency is usually just a synopsis of what's published on their blog.

It's worth noting that these news items can be useful if the blog post they're referring to is too long or hard to read. You'll probably discover that viewing interviews with founders and CEOs provides far more information about a project's future than its roadmap. If you're lucky, you'll come across a plan that includes realistic targets that can be met before the project runs out of funds or is destroyed by its rivals. If you're unlucky, you won't get a roadmap at all, and if the interviews you've watched don't give you the impression that the project will be around for a long time, you may be looking at a short-term investment. However, the future isn't everything. You must ensure that a project has delivered on its promises thus far. This is where the blog enters the picture. If you can't locate a blog on a cryptocurrency's website, you can often find it on their Medium page. Sometimes you have to go as far as their GitHub to see their progress, and that's when you should seriously consider whether the project is on shaky ground. Skimming over the headlines of a cryptocurrency project's blog is generally enough to get a sense of whether it has kept its word and where it is heading.

It's an excellent idea to read any key updates you come across, such as those relating to changes in tokenomics or major partnership announcements. If you don't find anything, don't dismiss it as a negative omen. The crypto media, like the mainstream media, has its own way of doing things and does not always cast light on the topics that need to be viewed. By this time, you should have all of the information you need to make an informed decision about whether a cryptocurrency is worthwhile. If you don't, you're probably dealing with a crypto project that you should be cautious of, if not avoid entirely. I'm sorry to say it, but this could also mean that you'll need to go back and take a closer look at the resources you used in your research. Doing your own bitcoin research can be time-consuming, but consider this: is a few hours of research worth a 100x or higher return on your investment? They are, indeed. When conducting cryptocurrency research, I first go to Coin Market Cap or Coin Gecko to determine if the token is being traded, especially on respected platforms. If it's not alive, it's not worth my time. Second, I visit YouTube to see what others are saying about the initiative. If they say something noteworthy, I make a few notes.

Next, I go to Messari and Binance Research to obtain a better understanding of the concept and how it operates. I next go to ICO Drops to examine how much money the project raised and how the tokens were distributed. I use the photographs they've provided, as well as Messari, to double-check that the information listed there is correct. Third, I revisit YouTube and watch nearly every recent interview with the project's CEO or founder. What they say frequently answers many of the questions I'd jotted down in the second phase. They also have a tendency to clarify any puzzling aspects of the technology that went over my head. I then looked to see if the cryptocurrency has a YouTube channel where I might get further information and explanations. Assuming that what I heard didn't turn me off, I move on to the fourth phase, which is to sift through the project's documentation. I search for any additional information about cryptocurrency technology, tokenomics, consensus methods, staking incentives, mining requirements, and any other basic components I've learned about so far.

Finally, I go over their roadmap and blog to check whether they've been making the progress they've promised and if they'll be able to serve what they say they'll be serving. I believe this is a fail-safe technique for conducting effective bitcoin research. It's the right combination of watching, reading, and repetition for me to ensure that what I've learned sticks in my head. It's easy to overlook that cryptocurrency is a very new subject that is still in its early stages. This means that if you can become proficient at conducting your own crypto research, you will be among the few individuals who understand what is going on when the retail Fomo begins to hit during this bull market. Not only will you make better investing selections as a result, but you may also be presented with chances beyond your wildest thoughts.

# CHAPTER 8:  WHAT ARE THE BEST PRACTICES FOR AVOID CRYPTO SCAMS

The quantity of scams that now infest the crypto world is one of the reasons why it can be so intimidating for newbies. Some are quite clear, while others are more subtle and nearly convincing. Scams must change in order to remain profitable, thus they are changing and have also been able to: con consumers who thought they were immune to it. Are any of these con games just around the corner? This chapter contains the comprehensive guide to crypto scams, as well as my top five list of ones to avoid. I'll also give you some pointers on how to prevent falling victim to scammers, hacks, and other foul techniques.

The first, and possibly most common, type of fraud I'd like to discuss is the ponzi scheme. This is actually far older than crypto, which dates back to the 1920s. It was named after Charles Ponzi, an Italian who used the strategy that carries his name to scam investors. A ponzi scheme's underlying principle is actually rather straightforward. An operator will typically pay out existing investors with funds raised from new investors. The company is not making any actual money. It creates the appearance of income, which may persuade many people who have invested that it is legitimate. This will continue indefinitely as long as there are fresh investors to bring in funds. Frequently, these schemes would also ask the user to refer others. This is why it's also known as a pyramid scheme.

Although the fundamentals of a Ponzi scheme are rather simple, some of them can be difficult to detect. Some ponzi schemes can run for years and deceive even the savviest investors. For example, Bernie Madoff ran one of the longest-running and most fraudulent ponzi schemes in history. His victims were sophisticated hedge funds, mutual funds, and high-net-worth individuals, not regular retail investors. Everyone agreed that Bernie was in high demand. There are waiting lists for him to invest with. Take a look at all the other wealthy people that believe in Bernie. They also adopt a slew of other guises or bogus commercial operations to justify their profits. They frequently strive to adopt approaches that appear to be plausible in order to avoid raising too many doubts. I won't go through all of them, but here are some of the most well-known front businesses for a ponzi scheme.

Platforms for crypto loans With them, you'll provide funds to a platform, and they'll give you a steady stream of interest. The implication is that there are borrowers on the opposite side of the equation who are paying that interest. On the surface, it appears to be a viable business concept. For example, during the Bitconnect era, they paid out monthly interest rates that approached 40%. This looked absurd and untenable, especially for a project as opaque as it was. Of course, we've all heard of Bitconnect's demise. Cloud mining is another common cryptocurrency ponzi scheme. The fraud will claim that your money is receiving a consistent return by mining cryptocurrencies. Of course, the money you invest is not used to purchase mining equipment, but rather to keep the plan running. There have been a few of these in the past, but the Bit Club network is likely the most well-known. They ran for more than five years and raised more than 720 million dollars from investors. Many people suspected them of being a ponzi scheme, but it was difficult to show definitely at the time that they were not putting the money in mining equipment.

The FBI, of course, had access to personal communications and eventually destroyed that ship. Another well-known cryptocurrency ponzi MO is an investment plan. They will either claim to be able to trade the crypto markets or to have some form of trading bot that can provide consistent returns. These are the types of ponzi schemes that are fairly simple to prevent. The truth is that any service that promises to offer a fantastic trading technique or the trading bot does not require your money. They might simply profit from their trading tactics. It's basically a ruse to obtain your money in order to pay off previous investors. There have been a few of these in the cryptocurrency field as well. Amfeix is one of the most recent examples. By the middle of 2020, they had earned about $60 million. That is until they used the money to conduct an exit scam. How do you avoid crypto ponzi schemes now that you have a hazy understanding of how they work? The first and most essential red flag to look for is if a program guarantees you a set amount of return.

Nothing is guaranteed, and comments like this should get your warning bells ringing. I know what you're thinking: your friend claims to have a consistent source of income month after month, and he most certainly does. This is the entire operation of a ponzi scheme. To persuade the investor that they do work and, as a result, wish to commit additional funds, the investor may even opt to suggest our friends and family. While we're on the subject, this is another red flag for a ponzi scheme. If the system promises you bonuses and privileges in exchange for referring people and tiers those referral levels, you should avoid it. This is multi-level marketing at its worst. Almost every crypto ponzi scheme in the past has used some variation of this. You would have high-profile promoters at the top of the pyramid who would profit from those below them. Don't be misled by marketing or public relations promoting a specific platform. Bitconnect promoted on Coindesk, Coin Market Cap, and a slew of other websites. They even purchased billboards. Ponzi schemes, like every other type of endeavor, are ad buyers. In fact, they are likely to spend more on advertising than legitimate firms since they require fresh victims. Many times, advertising networks, media sites, and influencers do not analyze the goods being advertised.

Consider a ponzi scheme to be an empty drum. Empty drums usually produce the most noise. The famed giveaway fraud is our next trick, and it is also rather popular. Simply put, the fraudster is attempting to persuade you to transfer the money in exchange for money that has been multiplied. Send us one BTC and we'll send you ten in return.

Despite how ridiculous that sounds, some con games are quite successful. They frequently pitch the marketing as a giveaway by a project influencer or other renowned person. They spread these scams through major social media networks.

Scammers were making over a million dollars in a spate of these giveaway promotions before Twitter cracked down on bot manipulation tactics. The Elon Musk ones were my personal favorite. They may be so convincing at times that major news organizations would fall for them. Twitter giveaway scams, on the other hand, have grown less popular as Twitter has cracked down on them. Scammers, on the other hand, have found fertile ground on YouTube. You've probably seen live stream giveaways where they feature an interview of some kind to encourage users to join. Users are directed to a website that provides instructions on where to transfer money and how it will be multiplied. These have proven to be pretty effective, and they've lately begun employing YouTube advertisements to display these videos.

Recently, it appears that YouTube has cracked down on some of these frauds, but they can surface in a variety of places, so it's critical that you can recognize and report them. They will try to disguise the message in some way. They may utilize forged transaction proof as well as time-sensitive pressure techniques. They will try to appeal to our emotional passion for fast gains and quick promotions, but you just have to take a step back and ask yourself, "Is it reasonable for someone to offer me free money over the internet?" That's a question I'm sure we all know the answer to.

The second scam that I must inform you of is a phishing scam. This is yet another attack vector that can be employed in a variety of ways. A phishing scam's ultimate purpose is to get you to hand over sensitive data so that a hacker can use that info to gain access to your cryptocurrency. Phishing scams are not limited to cryptocurrency and have been used to get access to people's online bank accounts, email accounts, and other password-protected services. A crypto phishing scheme's typical tactic is to convince you to visit a website that appears to be a real service. They could be in the form of an exchange, an online wallet, or any service that requires a password to access.

Scammers will frequently attempt to use a domain address that appears to be very near to the official URL of the site you're looking for. They will either rearrange a letter, include a hash, change the spelling, or use a new domain extension; dot net, dot info, and so on. The truly cunning will even go so far as to replace a letter with a number. For example, ledger.com with a 1 or ledger.com with an I in place of the l. It's quite convincing. The most skilled hackers will employ what are known as homograph attacks. These primarily make use of Unicode letters from non-Latin writing systems such as Cyrillic or Greek. They have the ability to make a domain look exactly like the desired one. These domains typically host sites that seem virtually identical to the site you intend to visit. This is almost certainly a login screen for the service in issue. You think you're logging into your account, but you're actually giving the scammer your information. They can access your accounts and, of course, do whatever they want with your Bitcoin once they get your login information.

Of course, there are safeguards you may take. One of them is to enable two-factor authentication, and while we're at it, avoid using SMS-based authentication. This is due to the fact that hackers can perform Sim swap attacks, allowing them to take control of your phone. Use Authy or Google Authenticator. Phishing attacks can be far more successful when the attackers also purchase ad space. Many times, they will run AdWords with a bogus domain, and Google would serve that in the search results.

Simply follow my basic rule of thumb: I never click on advertising, even if they aren't crypto-related. Private key phishing is an intriguing extension of phishing. If you're utilizing an online wallet, the scammer has an easy time with it. If you have a software wallet, however, they will have to convince you to download a malicious wallet, which is a fantastic segue into our following scan. Often, the scammer would employ phishing to trick you into downloading a malware wallet. Once you've done so, they'll want you to decrypt the wallet with the private key, which means they'll have access to all of your cryptocurrency. In 2020, perhaps the most damaging hack I heard about was a poor man who lost 1,400 Bitcoin. That's more than $21 million. It was primarily due to the user being duped into downloading a defective version of the wallet.

After installing a malware-infected wallet, the hackers gained remote control and stole the man's Bitcoin. Essentially, if you're using a wallet on your computer, make sure you get it from the official site. Make certain that it is on the domain that corresponds to the wallet in question. Don't fall for bogus domain attacks. When downloading these wallet files, you can add another degree of security by using what is known as a checksum. Essentially, this is where you can validate the digital signatures that the developer has included with the software. This is intended for more technical users who are familiar with the command line. It's also worth noting that this isn't limited to wallets downloaded from the official site. There have also been reports of fraudulent wallets being posted to centralized app stores. As an example, consider the recent occurrences of a bogus Metamask wallet that was posted to the Chrome browser store. Scammers will even create bogus ratings and comments to make the browser wallet appear legitimate. You're probably assuming that because you utilize a hardware wallet, you're not vulnerable to these hacks. That may not be totally correct. If you own a ledger device, there's a good chance you've heard about the ledger database breach.

Essentially, hackers gained access to the data of about 200,000 Ledger users, including emails, names, phone numbers, and so on. However, I must emphasize that this was not a hack of the real Ledger device, and there are no weaknesses in those. However, the data may have been utilized to execute a phishing attack against Ledger device owners. A few months ago, the hackers sold the data on the dark web. Scammers bought the data, and it was only a matter of time before we saw those focused phishing attempts known as spear phishing. Users have received emails and SMS messages informing them that they must update their Ledger firmware or Ledger live. Of course, they'll send the customer to a phony domain similar to the ones I mentioned.

As with other wallet viruses, once you've downloaded the forge ledger live, it will exfiltrate your seed words and steal your cryptocurrency faster than you can say Bitcoin. The only place you should update your Ledger is from within the app. All changes will be delivered straight to the app by Ledger. Aside from this spear phishing attempt, criminals have utilized other approaches, which I've mentioned for new Ledger users. They either published bogus Ledger apps to respective app marketplaces or ran AdWords campaigns using Ledger-related keywords. By the way, this isn't exclusive to Ledger. Other hardware devices, such as Trezor and Keepkey, have also been targeted by scammers. You're probably wondering if hardware devices are still safe. Well, that's what I think. They're far safer than many alternatives, and even in the event of the Ledger breach, the device had nothing to do with it. Over at Ledger, there was a lack of data security. You're already two steps ahead of the hackers if you're aware of the attempts to fish.

On to the next scan, and this one is a doozy. Rug pulls and exit scams are not limited to ponzi schemes; they have also been employed effectively in fraudulent ICOs. It is not difficult to grasp how these scams work. They attempt to persuade a user to purchase a cryptocurrency in an Initial Coin Offering. They expect that by doing so, they can gain momentum and attract additional people. Once they've gathered a sufficient number of users, they'll cut and flee, leaving everyone else holding the bag. During the 2017 ICO frenzy, ICO variants of these were all over the place. A lot of high-profile ICOs were able to pull off daring exit schemes. However, as interest in ICOs has recently decreased, scammers have picked a new target. Given the increasing interest in the DeFi space, scammers have recently transferred their approaches to these waters. They'll develop a new protocol, usually a fork of an existing one, and then provide their own token as a yield farming incentive to get others to contribute capital to the system. When they achieve critical mass, the developers abandon the token and flee with some of the locked capital. It is also rather straightforward to prevent these types of scams. Avoid becoming engaged in the first place. There is a lot more garbage out there than great projects with promising futures. Even if an ICO or DeFi protocol is not a hoax, there is a good probability that a smart contract issue exists.

One that exposes the protocol to a hack or other catastrophic failure. When it comes to picking the correct projects to invest in or techniques to yield a farm, I am quite picky. Most of these touted ICOs and initiatives should be treated as if they were drugs. Simply say no. Some scams are quite massive, in that they target thousands of users. This is true of the ponzi schemes I outlined previously. Scammers, on the other hand, will sometimes pay you special attention. They will spend more time with you, attempting to gain your trust and, ideally, gaining access to your money.

The primary premise of this fraud is that there is someone who can assist you trade, mining, or earning cryptocurrencies in some way. They'll try a variety of methods to entice users to contact them. This will be done via email or a messaging app such as WhatsApp or Telegram. For example, if you've recently been scouting some of the crypto YouTube comments, you'll have noticed a surge of fraudulent comments. Bot likes and comments are commonly used to exaggerate these figures. The comments either discuss a trader, a hacker, or cryptocurrencies. They spread quickly, which I can only assume means they're successful. It's also difficult to stop the scammers because all they're doing is utilizing an email or phone number to persuade you to hand over your cryptocurrency. It's a modern take on the Nigerian prince email hoax. Spam emails from a distant prince wanting to transfer your money that he needs to get out of the country.

Similar to the giveaway hoax, you must ask yourself if it makes sense. You transfer someone money over the internet, and they offer to make more money for you. What could possibly go wrong, right? The truth is that they are only the tip of the iceberg when it comes to frauds. The best con artists are those who are continuously coming up with new ways to defraud people. They all, however, have a similar strategy. They're playing on your greed or your fear. They expect you to make a rapid judgement without thinking things through thoroughly. I always employ a simple rule of thumb: does it sound too good to be true? Well, if it does then you can be pretty confident it is. When it comes to phishing and wallet frauds, you just need to be cautious when downloading wallet software and visiting specific websites. Being forewarned is being forearmed.

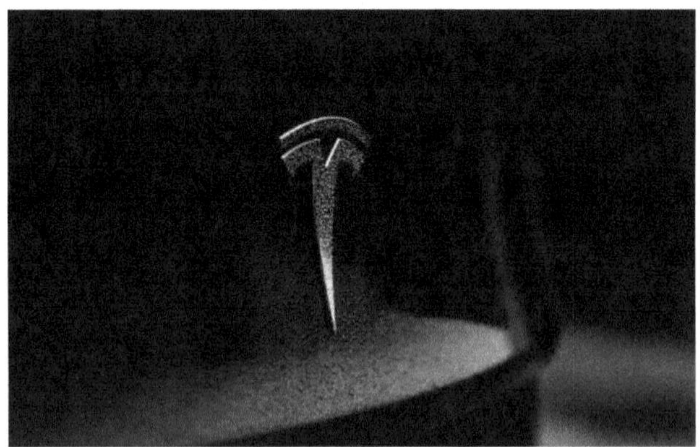

# CHAPTER 9:  HOW TO TRADE BITCOIN VS TESLA

Bitcoin is a high-risk investment. It has the highest volatility of any asset class. Its valuation is illogical. These are all statements I've heard about Bitcoin. All of these are preconceptions promoted by the mainstream media. So this got me thinking about what might happen if I looked into the stock market. Is it possible that there are equities that match the media's definition of Bitcoin? Tesla is many things: an automaker's villain, a car manufacturer with tech stock prices, and so on. It is, without a question, a divisive organization, but I believe it perfectly represents the feared Bitcoin risks.

This is quite high for a stock of any denomination, let alone one with a market capitalization of $661 billion. In comparison, Bitcoin's 30-day realized volatility is only 21%. This is for a cryptocurrency with a market capitalization of $1.02 trillion. We all know that past performance does not predict future results. Similarly, prior volatility cannot be predicted to persist in the future. The option implied volatility, on the other hand, might give you a good picture of what traders estimate the volatility to be. This is the volatility that is priced into options, and it is possible that it is the best predictor of what realized volatility will be. What are our thoughts on Tesla stock options? Well, Tesla's 30-day implied volatility is more than 102 percent. On the Bitcoin front, the implied volatility of a 30-day option is only approximately 50%.

Bitcoin option buyers factor in less volatility than Tesla option traders. What does it all mean? Essentially, Tesla is a far riskier investment than Bitcoin. Not only based on historical performance, but also on predicted volatility, and it's not just Bitcoin. If we look at Ethereum, the second most valued cryptocurrency, realized volatility is 44 percent and implied volatility is 54 dollars. As a result, it is obvious that Tesla is objectively more statistically volatile than Bitcoin. However, financial markets are all about the risk-reward tradeoff. Do you believe Tesla's risk premium is reasonable in light of potential future rewards? I don't, and it's based on some solid fundamental analysis, so let's look at that now. People tend to value a firm in a variety of ways. Multiple valuations are one of the most tried and tested methods. These are essentially measures of a company's pricing as a ratio of some of its financial parameters. We're talking about multiples like price to earnings or PE, price to sales or PS, and so on. It is essentially a measure of how much investors place on a dollar of earnings or sales generated by the company. These are only truly useful in terms of determining how a company is valued in comparison to other companies in the same market. Over at Tesla, based on a five-dollar adjusted EPS for 2020. The forward PE ratio is greater than 326 times. To put it another way, 326 years of earnings are required to support the current share price of about $1600. To put this in context, the typical PE ratio for a vehicle firm is approximately 6.87 times. Some may argue that price to profits is not the ideal multiple to utilize in this case.

They argue that price to sales is a better metric because Tesla is more of a technology firm. It's debatable whether that makes sense, but let's pretend for the sake of argument that it was to be valued using those parameters. Tesla has a forward price to sales ratio of around 11 times based on an estimated sales projection. How does this compare to other tech firms? Amazon, on the other hand, has a price-to-sales ratio of 4.3. Google has a ratio of 6.9:1. Facebook has a 9.1 rating. Is Tesla going to outperform these companies in terms of growth and hence demand such a high valuation? Indeed, the entire earnings growth argument has been utilized to explain Tesla's exorbitant multiples.

Analysts believe that Tesla will be able to grow its sales quicker than all competitors, which is why it deserves such a high price. Let's take a closer look at that. I don't own a Tesla, but I've ridden in quite a few of them. They are, nonetheless, a really amazing piece of equipment. However, one must set aside their personal consumer preferences and examine the situation objectively. Do you believe that demand for battery electric vehicles will increase, especially in the midst of the current global recession? Particularly given that hybrid vehicles are far less expensive than BEVs and could provide a cost-effective alternative for people to purchase an ecologically sustainable vehicle.

Even if individuals were dead set on acquiring a BEV, couldn't they go for a less expensive model like a Nissan Leaf or a Volvo xc40? Warren Buffett frequently discusses the importance of building a defensive moat around your organization. That gives you a competitive advantage, making it tough for your competitors to take your market share. Tesla has name brand value, but it is not an impenetrable fortress. There is a case that can be made for scale economics. Many Tesla supporters believe that when further production at the gigafactories ramps up, cars will become much more affordable. They point to the Shanghai gigafactory as an example of how economies of scale can be obtained in a country, and although this is undeniably true, the same experience cannot be expected in other countries where Tesla is considering building a gigafactory.

One of these locations is the gigafactory, which is being developed outside of Berlin. The German labor market is far tighter than China's. Wages are undoubtedly greater, and all employees are unionized. Unlike in the United States, where unions are weak, or in China, where unions simply do not exist, unions in Germany are strong and effective. Did you know, for example, that in 2017, a union called IG Metal was able to secure a 30 percent raise at a Tesla-owned car parts manufacturer? The gigafactory in Berlin will employ 12,000 people, most of whom will be unionized.

Isn't it possible that if this union was able to win concessions from Tesla for a much smaller operation, they could try to force Tesla's hand at the Berlin factory? After all, unions cherish their authority, and this is assuming that everything remains steady on a macroeconomic basis. Regardless of how much many would like to believe that we are done with the coronavirus, it is not. The last thing many people were thinking about was what kind of new car they should get. They were likely to buy you then had ramifications for the broader economy and supply chain disruption - not the best economic situation for a car maker. Not to mention another aspect of the economic fallout: governments are highly indebted. As a result, they are far less inclined to provide large subsidies for electric vehicles. Fewer subsidies mean fewer incentives to acquire electric vehicles, particularly those that are more expensive than much of the competition.

So, in my opinion, the concept that Tesla can reach those remarkable growth statistics to justify its price is, at best, doubtful. Don't misunderstand me. I'm not a Tesla detractor. I believe the company's history is profound, and Elon Musk is a rather groundbreaking figure. However, at these costs, Tesla simply does not make sense. Less sense than Bitcoin, which is a natural segue into the following issue. I know there are many "no coiners" out there who would never consider investing in cryptocurrencies, and that's fine. Everyone has different perspectives, and they should invest depending on their main abilities. The valuation of a cryptocurrency is far more intricate than the valuation of a firm. You don't have financial reports or sales figures to rely on.

Other indicators pertaining to scarce assets and decentralized networks must be considered. I'm going to start with Bitcoin and use the well-known stock to flow model. This is a model that attempts to value Bitcoin as if it were a scarce commodity with limited supply. Technically, this is what Bitcoin is. It's a resource with a maximum supply of 21 million that must be mined. Furthermore, the more that are mined, the more difficult the mining becomes. Every few years, the amount of new Bitcoin entering the market is reduced by a process known as halving, and we recently saw one in May when Bitcoin inflation was cut in half. The model itself was created by a guy known as Plan B, and it has sparked a lot of interest in the crypto community. The raw statistical analysis of the model is outside the scope of this book, but here's the gist of it: Commodity prices are determined by the amount of available supply and the rate at which new supply enters the market. The greater the stock-to-flow ratio, the longer it will take to achieve the entire supply. For example, gold has a ratio of 62; prior to the halving, Bitcoin had a ratio of 25, but it has subsequently risen to 56. This effectively means that Bitcoin is becoming more scarce. It will be scarcer than gold when we reach the next halving event. That is one of the primary investing scenarios for Bitcoin. When you own Bitcoin, you are a member of an exclusive group known as the 21 million clubs, and here's an interesting tidbit.

According to a Credit Suisse Global Wealth study, the world has 46 million millionaires. This means that there would be insufficient Bitcoin to go around if everyone wanted one. Could they put their money into gold? True, but gold is difficult to store, transport, or sell. Would you attempt to cross a border with a billion dollars in gold? While a little Ledger device can access a billion dollars worth of Bitcoin. In fact, the Ledger isn't even required. With a brain wallet, you can literally store billions of dollars in your head. So the scarcity argument is compelling, and it is the major motivator behind the stock-to-flow concept. Based on calculations, the model has some rather bold predictions for what Bitcoin's price could be by the end of the year. This could be especially important in light of the massive monetary and fiscal stimulus that has recently entered the market.

Stimulus that may have had a direct impact on the valuation of companies like Tesla. To say the least, the response of governments and central bankers to shore up global economies is extraordinary. Trillions of dollars, euros, and pounds have been poured into the ecosystem. Some of this money has been loaned out by central banks.

Some of it has gone to corporations and Wall Street organizations, and a substantial portion of it has gone to individuals through government checks. While much of this money was used to see individuals through to better times, a large portion of them began to use some of these funds to trade equities. They selected to trade on a variety of equities. These included not only Tesla but also a number of other companies, including Nikola, a truck manufacturer with no income, indicating that government stimulus money has certainly distorted the stock markets. When the FED printed additional money out of thin air, it allowed Wall Street to profit from higher money supply chasing capital investments.

In a pandemic, more bankers are making money. But you're probably wondering what this has to do with Bitcoin. Simply put it is inflation. While inflation may not be a major problem right now, it will undoubtedly rear its ugly head once we are free of these lockdowns. All of this free money is now in the system, and when consumer spending returns, there will be more money chasing finite commodities. Bitcoin is a fundamentally limited supply asset. It, like gold, can be viewed as an inflation hedge. It is a store of value unaffected by Jerome and his money printing machine. While government regulations may artificially boost the value of Tesla and other equities, Bitcoin is governed solely by code. The private keys are completely decentralized, borderless, and in the hands of individuals who have them. I believe I've sung Bitcoin's praises sufficiently, but I am far from a Bitcoin maximalist, which is why I also hold a large portion of my assets in Ethereum. This programmable cryptocurrency has its own distinct investment case, which I'd like to discuss. The theory's central tenet is that Eth is valuable because the more the network is used, the greater the demand for the cryptocurrency that drives the network. This is the utility demand, which is fueled by DAP developers, enterprise networks, tokenized stable currency, DiFi protocols, and a big user base. To get a feel of how much utility demand there is on the network, just look at the growth of the DiFi sector, the amount of Ethereum transactions, and the number of unique addresses. Furthermore, with the future release of Ethereum 2.0, protocol users will be able to stake. They are not only investing in a protocol with enormous usefulness, but they are also investing in an asset with a consistent return. All of this adds to its value. These staking returns are paid to network participants and can be compared to guaranteed dividends on a stock. Dividends are not required for stocks, and some corporations do not pay them at all. To be fair to Tesla, they do not have earnings to disperse because they have only recently become successful and choose to invest their profits in further growth. This is the method used by a number of other digital companies, but the point I'm trying to make is that once Ethereum 2.0 is released, users will not only benefit from the protocol's worth, but they will also reap the benefits of regular returns through staking.

The staking component is merely one part of the overall upgrading. There are also several more savings and enhancements that will allow the Ethereum network to scale to thousands of transactions per second. According to the fat protocol theory, all of this makes the Ethereum protocol more interesting for development and hence enhances its value. Finally, this isn't just my opinion on Ethereum. A number of significant and well-heeled institutional investors have staked their Eth in anticipation of the launch. They are diversifying their Bitcoin holdings, demonstrating that different cryptocurrencies are not mutually exclusive. The pandemic and economic response have clearly flipped the world upside down. Not only in how we function in our daily lives, but also in how we invest. Tesla has long been a trader's favorite, but the new infusion of stimulus funds has made it much riskier. Aside from the daily price volatility, the price itself does not make sense based on most valuation indicators. Those multiples must be justified. You have to trust that Tesla will significantly increase its sales and earnings. People are looking to buy pricey electric vehicles in the midst of one of the worst economic recessions in our lifetimes, you have to believe. My Bitcoin investment, on the other hand, makes a lot more sense. It is a precious global asset that only a few people may own.

A type of asset that can be used to hold billions of dollars on a simple hardware wallet or piece of paper. Digital gold, which is governed by code and is resistant to censorship, will take on a whole new gold identity when the inevitable inflation begins to bite. It's my insurance policy against things over which I have no control. In terms of price projection, when it comes to Tesla, the stock market is almost certain to re-enter bear market territory by the end of the year. If this is the case, hot stocks such as Tesla are expected to fall in value. I expect Tesla to decrease by at least 30%, resulting in a share price of at least $500. This results in a price-to-earnings ratio of 98 times and a price-to-sales ratio of three times. This would still be high for its industry, but much more fair when compared to contemporaries in the technology sector, such as Amazon. On the Bitcoin side, I won't say I completely agree with the stock to flow model, but its fundamental economics make sense. The model estimates that Bitcoin will be worth $75,000 by the end of the year. That seems a little optimistic to me, but I wouldn't be shocked. These are only my predictions.

# CHAPTER 10:   HOW TO INVEST IN DECENTRALIZED ICO-S

In the crypto realm, there have been over 5,700 ICOs. The majority of these occurred during the ICO booms in 2017 and 2018, with over $6 billion raised in 2017. Only a few of those 5,000+ projects have delivered on their promises, and several of those debuted their main nets only in 2020, and now it's Filecoin's moment to shine. It's been more than four years since Filecoin's pre-sale and ICO, which raised more than a quarter-billion dollars, and now Filecoin's mainnet is finally here. So, in this chapter, I'll tell you about a crypto project that fuels the economy of a new decentralized internet that is owned and operated by everyone and could potentially be utilized in other worlds. Protocol Labs created Filecoin, a decentralized storage network. Protocol Labs is a network protocol research and development firm situated in San Francisco. It was launched in 2014 by Stanford graduate Juan Bennett and got over $3 million in funding from the renowned YCombinator business accelerator program. One is the CEO of Protocol Labs, which has expanded from a dozen to over 130 employees since its inception. Protocol Labs' ultimate goal is to build a fast, secure, and decentralized internet.

Today's internet is incredibly centralized. All of the web content with which you interact is stored on centralized servers, which can experience outages or be shut down if they house content that someone with big guns, large pockets, or both don't want others to see. The trade-off is that these centralized internet providers provide most of us with fast, high-quality internet connections at a low cost. Previously, decentralized solutions were not possible because they were either too slow, too expensive, or both. As a result, Protocol Labs created two solutions to address these difficulties and provide the framework for a functional, fast, cost-effective, and user-friendly web 3.0. The initial product, the Interplanetary File System (IPFS), was published in 2015. It enables anyone to accept and host web content in a similar fashion to BitTorrent. The IPFS was created to function similarly to the internet that we are all familiar with. In other words, the front end of an IPFS website looks and feels like any other http website. At the start of 2020, the IPFS has over 5 billion files. Because the IPFS is based on a network of nodes rather than centralized servers, it will be feasible to provide a high-quality internet experience on other planets in the future. This is due to the elimination of the need to repeatedly refer back to centralized internet servers on Earth, which can take minutes or even hours depending on which planet you're on.

The second product is Filecoin, a decentralized storage blockchain established in 2017 and built on the IPFS protocol. Its role is to act as an incentive layer to maintain and build the IPFS by paying individuals who assist in file storage and retrieval using Filecoin's native Fil currency. Filecoin hopes to compete with centralized cloud storage providers such as Amazon and Google in addition to supporting IPFS. This puts Filecoin in direct rivalry with other decentralized data storage cryptocurrencies such as Sia coin and Storj. After more than three years of development, Filecoin's mainnet became operational on October 15th, 2020. This was followed by file coin liftoff, which was essentially a one-week celebration. There were dozens of online panels, workshops, and speeches regarding Filecoin and web 3.0. But how exactly does Filecoin work? Filecoin operates in the same way that most other cryptocurrencies do. It has a blockchain, a consensus mechanism, mining, and mining rewards are paid in its own native cryptocurrency.

The Filecoin blockchain is based on the IPFS protocol. There are no files stored on the blockchain. It serves as the Ledger for filling transactions and the balances of Filecoin wallet addresses. The Filecoin blockchain also contains the agreements established between the miners who store client data and the clients who requested the storage of that data. Two Consensus Mechanisms are used on the Filecoin network. The first Consensus Mechanism is known as proof of replication, and it entails demonstrating that a specific piece of data is being stored by a miner. When a miner creates a data storage contract with a client, he or she must add this proof to the Filecoin blockchain.

The second Consensus Mechanism is known as proof of space-time, and it entails confirming that a miner is still storing data. Every time a client or other network participant asks if they're still storing that data, a miner must post this proof to the Filecoin blockchain. The mining of Filecoin is where things become interesting. In contrast to mining Bitcoin, Ethereum, or any other proof-of-work cryptocurrency, all you need to mine Filecoin is a good computer, a stable internet connection, and lots of hard drive space. This is due to the fact that your goal as a Filecoin miner is not to burn a circuit with your improvised Asic mining farm but to store a massive amount of encrypted user data on a thick HDD. You'll also need to stake some Fil tokens in addition to the hardware. This is done to keep you on your best behavior. If you are discovered to have breached the terms of your contract with a client, such as deleting the data before the agreed-upon deadline, your collateral may be reduced in part.

The precise amount of fill you must pay is proportionate to the amount of storage you provide as a percentage of the network. For example, if you're holding one terabyte of data for a client, which is one percent of the entire storage available on the Filecoin network, your Fil stake must be one percent of the total Fil currently staked. This increases the security of the blockchain by tying the cost of corruption not just to the number of fill tokens you have, but also to the amount of hardware you're packing. As more miners join, it gets more expensive to corrupt the Filecoin network. Because the cost of the Fil you need to stake to become a miner might be fairly high in some cases, Filecoin provides two staking methods. You can either put down the collateral upfront or choose to put down less collateral and use a percentage of your future block earnings as collateral. Block rewards on Filecoin are determined by the network's size.

The more the Filecoin network expands, the more Fil tokens are available in each block. This is done to encourage network growth and to ensure that miners are suitably compensated in the future. Each miner's block reward is proportionate to the amount of storage space he or she contributes to the network. As with staking, if you provide 1% of the total storage available on Filecoin, you will receive 1% of all block rewards. It is important to note that as a miner, you will earn these block rewards just by participating in the Filecoin network. Consider it your starting salary in a sales position. The commission is the Fil tokens you receive directly from clients in exchange for agreeing to store their data. Depending on network conditions and the size of your hard drive, this can make becoming a Filecoin miner pretty profitable. Now that you understand the Filecoin principle, let's look at an application. Assume you have a terabyte of solely educational information that you want to save on Filecoin. The first step is to locate a decentralized storage app.

These are similar to Ethereum decentralized applications, only they're built on top of Filecoin, and because Filecoin is built on top of IPFS, decentralized storage applications appear and feel like conventional websites. Furthermore, they do not require the use of a web 3.0 wallet such as Metamask. They are literally the simple front-end application you use, while the Filecoin network does all the heavy lifting in the background. These decentralized storage solutions will enable you to determine the terms of your data storage contract. This covers the lifetime of the contract, how many times you want the data to be replicated when it's stored, and how much you're prepared to pay in Fil tokens for those circumstances. You can even specify the specific storage miners you want to use. Assuming you didn't set an unreasonably low price for your demands, a storage miner will accept the conditions of your contract to store your data. The acceptance of the contract is written to the Filecoin blockchain, along with the new balance of Fil tokens in your and the storage miners' wallets. Every so often, the Filecoin network will ask the miners storing your data to submit proof that they are still storing your educational content, lest their stake is slashed. Suppose that it's time to break out the educational content. When you request to retrieve the data you've stored using the decentralized storage application, a signal is sent out behind the scenes to retrieval miners. These may or may not also be storage miners. As the name suggests, retrieval miners are tasked with retrieving your data as quickly as possible. Naturally, they aren't going to do this for free. You're going to have to shell out some Fil token. This cost depends on how desperate you are to study. If you're patient, it will cost you next to nothing. If you need your educational content right this minute, it will cost you more. Once your data is retrieved, you simply download it back to your device and you're studying away. You might be wondering how Filecoin compares to other decentralized storage crypto projects like Sia.

Without drowning you with the details, it all comes down to two things scale and economics. Sia and Storj are simply looking to store user data in a decentralized manner and market their projects as a way to make money from the extra hard drive space you might have lying around. In contrast, Filecoin is just one piece of the Protocol Labs puzzle. Filecoin is not just looking to store user data, but it wants to become the storage layer for all web 3.0 data, even data from other cryptocurrency blockchains. In fact, the Protocol Labs team envisions a future where all the data from decentralized applications built on Ethereum and other smart contract blockchains, is stored using the Filecoin network. That is the scale the project is going for and it's a big part of why it took so long for the Filecoin main net to launch. In 2020 Sia had to add a layer 2 solution called Skynet to fix its scaling issues, despite storing only a fraction of the data which Filecoin aims to support. On the other hand, Filecoin's scale might just be its achilles heel as both Sia and especially Storj have lower barriers to entry to participate on their networks, in terms of hardware and stake. This could limit the sort of network participation Filecoin will require, if it wants to grow to the size that Protocol Labs is aiming for. This brings us to economics. Filecoin has a massive war chest. To understand just how massive, Filecoin raised almost 10 times more capital than Sia coin and Storj combined. Money goes a long way when it comes to marketing and adoption, especially when you're trying to appeal to institutions and not just your average guy. I highly doubt Protocol Labs has spent all of that money over the last three years. Filecoin also already has nearly double the number of active storage providers than Sia, and a storage capacity this is 300 times larger. This is relevant because it means that if you're looking to store data on Filecoin you will probably be able to do so for a good price, at least for the time being. This is because a large amount of storage volume and storage miners compared to clients increases the likelihood that they will compete to store your data. Contrast this to Sia coin where storage fees are relatively fixed, albeit still very competitive compared to centralized data storage providers like Amazon and Google.

Filecoin has also put a lot of thought into its tokenomics, so let's now look at just that. Fil is Filecoin's native token. No ERC20 shenanigans here. It's a deflationary asset since Fil tokens are burned to pay for network fees or whenever a storage miner stake is slashed. Fil has a maximum supply of 2 billion, with an initial supply of 600 million. Of this total supply 70 percent has been set aside for Filecoin miners, 15 percent will go to Protocol Labs, 7.5 percent was sold during the 2017 ICO, 2.5 percent has been allocated to future fundraising and ecosystem development, and the last 5 percent was reserved for the Filecoin foundation. The Fil tokens allocated to Protocol Labs and the Filecoin foundation have a six-year linear vesting schedule, whereas the tokens sold during the ICO are gradually vested with every Filecoin block that's mined and may last anything from six months to three years.

The Filecoin ICO caused a bit of controversy in the crypto space. This is because it was only open to accredited investors in the United States. This meant that the only people who are allowed to participate were those with more than a million dollars in the bank or an annual income of more than 200,000 US dollars. You can imagine my shock then when I opened up one of Filecoin's block explorers and saw that most storage miners on the Filecoin network are apparently located in Singapore. What's more, is that the Filecoin foundation and Protocol Labs appear to have all their allocated tokens already. Thankfully they don't seem to have sold any. It's unclear whether these tokens are locked in a smart contract, or if they're currently accessible by both parties - An important question to say the least. Not much is known about the Filecoin foundation. This is problematic because Protocol Labs appears to be giving them the authority of Filecoin at some time in the future. In any event, Filecoin has detailed the three economic stages through which the network will pass. In a word, as the network increases, the emission rate of Fil tokens will decrease considerably. One final point I'd want to mention is Filecoin's future. Filecoin does not appear to have a clear plan. They do have a timeline that began in March of 2020 and appears to conclude with the introduction of the mainnet. It is possible that they will change it, so keep a watch on their website.

The lack of a defined timeline is hardly surprising given that it is really simply a cog in Protocol Labs' much larger aim to create a new decentralized internet via IPFS. That being said, I believe I have a good sense of what Filecoin might do next. During my study, I came upon the Filecoin enhancement proposal Github repository. According to what I've learned, Filecoin community members will soon be able to submit a Filecoin enhancement proposal. This is something new, as the Github source for FIPS does not provide many specifics on how to submit one or what the voting conditions will be, if any.

Given the crypto trend of moving to a decentralized autonomous organization, I wouldn't be surprised if Filecoin followed suit. However, the fact that Protocol Labs just modified Fil token incentives to satisfy irate storage miners makes me reconsider. We'll just have to wait and see. That's all there is to Filecoin. Although this chapter provided you with a bird's-eye view of Filecoin, what's happening in the grass is susceptible to change. To put it another way, many aspects of this project are still being worked out. Some of these are critical to understand, while others may alter. Now that that's out of the way, here's my take on Filecoin. Filecoin is a blockchain that is constructed on top of IPFS, a decentralized alternative to the centralized http internet. By paying contributors of storage space to the new decentralized web with Fil tokens, Filecoin provides economic incentives. It aspires to be the web 3.0 data storage layer, holding all data from decentralized websites and applications regardless of blockchain. Despite a few small hiccups with Fil token allocation and emission, the Filecoin mainnet has been robust from the start, providing the most storage space of any existing decentralized data storage provider on the market. While a specific strategy has not been finalized, Filecoin appears keen to collaborate with its community after spending years creating its network under investor pressure. One of the largest ICOs in cryptocurrency history has concluded, and there is much to show for it.

# CHAPTER 11: HOW TO INVEST AND TRADE CRYPTOCURRENCY IPO

If you thought 2021 was a wild ride in the crypto markets, you're in for a big surprise. A different kind of wave will arrive in 2022, one with a typical finance bent. Of course, I'm referring to the year of the crypto business IPO. In this chapter, I'll tell you everything you need to know about these prospective ICOs. What companies are doing them when they are doing them, whether to invest and what it implies for the markets What's the deal with all this IPO nonsense? Surely, we should be discussing ICOs and DEX offerings.

After all, this is crypto. That's because cryptocurrency companies are now taking their fundraising efforts to the next level. They're thinking about going in the usual route of an Initial Public Offering, or IPO. For example, you've probably heard that your favorite cryptocurrency exchange plans to go public next year. The Securities and Exchange Commission received Coinbase's draft registration statement on Form S-1. When a firm decides to go public, this is the first stage. It was unsurprising given how much the exchange has expanded in the last year. However, it appears that the timing was perfectly planned, with the event occurring about the same time as Bitcoin is breaking all-time highs. There is undeniably a lot of buzz surrounding cryptocurrency in the traditional financial sector. Having the option to hold shares in a company at the forefront of the crypto markets is something that these investors would not want to pass up, and despite what you may think about Coinbase, there is a reason why these shares could be in great demand. It ultimately comes down to the exchange's profitability. While you may believe the exchange fees you must pay to be excessive, they do benefit Coinbase's bottom line. Coinbase is banking as long as there is a volume in the crypto markets. Fees are accrued whether there is a buying or selling pressure. The only time they lose money is when market volatility causes their servers to fail. The timing is not by chance.

The primary purpose of an IPO is to raise as much capital as possible for the company in question. They are attempting to maximize their worth, which necessitates launching at a moment when there is a lot of buzz about the firm and sector in question. There is no better moment to invest in cryptocurrency than now. That's all well and good, but what kind of price could Coinbase fetch, and could it be a compelling diversification bet beyond simply holding crypto? According to Massari's account, they ran a handful of statistics to figure out what kind of valuation Coinbase could command in the IPO. This research is carried out using certain well-known financial indicators used to appraise organizations. These are valuation multiples, such as price-to-sales ratios. To begin with, you can be very certain that the company will be more valuable than it was in its most recent funding round. That occurred in October of 2018 when they raised 308 million dollars in their series E funding round. This put Coinbase's post-money valuation at around $8 billion. Based on 2018 revenue predictions, that would suggest a price-to-sales ratio of around 6.2 times. What's important to remember here is that 2018 was the pinnacle of the crypto bear market. An exchange gets money from fees, and if people aren't trading, they don't make any, so it's fairly incredible that Coinbase was able to make nearly 1.3 billion dollars in revenue when the rest of the market was still licking its wounds, and it's not just income. Profit estimates for that year are at $456 million, indicating that they are a highly profitable firm. Most people are aware that high-growth startups do not generate a profit because they are primarily focused on growth. Uber is still losing money despite the fact that it was listed over a year ago and has been in operation since 2009. They only hope to break even by the end of 2021.

All of this means that when Coinbase does go public, it will almost certainly command a high price-to-sales ratio. That series erasure occurred nearly two years ago in a very difficult market environment. Can you picture what their numbers will be in 2020, one of the most transformative years of all? We know that two things are likely to have increased: revenue and the premium investors are ready to pay on that revenue price to sales. Because Coinbase is a private corporation, financial statements have yet to be provided. Massari, on the other hand, has created a financial model that they will use to forecast revenue in 2020. They basically break into each of Coinbase's business areas and attempt to forecast most likely income. This is determined by factors such as known user numbers, volume, and fees. Based on their forecast, Coinbase's full-year revenue for 2020 is anticipated to be 1.6 billion. Not an outlandish figure, especially given the year we've had. Now that we have a revenue estimate, we must determine the most appropriate multiple that may be applied to the revenue. Comparables are frequently utilized in traditional equity valuations to arrive at this multiple.

Of course, it's difficult to acquire specifics on these comparables because there haven't been many crypto companies like Coinbase listed on the open market. However, there is now only one example of a listed crypto exchange service, and that is the Hong Kong-listed BC Technology Group. The Massari model relied on their financial statements to calculate a likely multiple that can be applied to the Coinbase exchange business – a three-year average of this ratio is 19.9 times. Because using a single company to calculate a multiple is problematic, Massari looked at some of the multiples that can be backed out from traditional financial companies. Companies like Stock Exchange Operators and Custodians, because their business structures are comparable to Coinbase's. Based on these firms, they estimated a price-to-sale ratio of 12.7 times for exchanges and two times for four custodians. With an average, we have a price-to-sales ratio of around 12 times. As a result, the range of coin basis valuation is estimated to be between 32 billion based on a multiple of 19.9 and 19 billion based on a ratio of 12. Massari has zeroed in on this further by performing a probability weighted valuation between the two ratios, yielding our grand total of 28 billion dollars. Those fees appear to be doing very well for the exchange. Of course, because this is a model, it is only an estimate. When Coinbase releases their financials before listing, we will all have a better understanding of what they are. It's also worth noting that no one knows the exact multiple it could command.

When compared to some of the other tech unicorns that are currently on the market, 17 times is a tad on the high side. For example, Airbnb is seeking a valuation of $47 billion, which is around ten times its 2019 revenue. It's not profitable, and we all know that Airbnb has had a rough year. If Coinbase is profitable and holds its IPO at the same time as all of the other excitement in the crypto markets, the valuation may skyrocket. There is, in fact, a crypto futures market for Coinbase shares that has started up. The Maverick FTX exchange listed Coinbase share perpetuals not long after the announcement of the Coinbase IPO. Each contract's price is essentially the possible Coinbase market cap divided by 250 million. The contracts are currently selling for $250. This means that the futures market's implied market cap is 62 billion dollars. The cryptocurrency markets can be crazy at times, pushing prices to unsustainable levels. Even if the crypto markets go crazy, I don't think Coinbase will command that price, but it does illustrate that when Coinbase does ultimately go public, there will be plenty of ordinary investors yearning to buy-in. If Coinbase is successful in its IPO, we may expect a deluge of similar filings to reach the market.

A chain reaction of crypto firms taking advantage of cheap finance. But what other firms might be thinking about? Bitmain has long hoped to go public. The mining chip manufacturer first considered a Hong Kong IPO in 2018. That appeared to fail, as the application expired in March 2019. Not to be deterred, it was reported at the end of last year that Bitmain had surreptitiously filed with the US Securities and Exchange Commission. This was done in preparation for their US IPO, which would have made them one of the largest Bitcoin mining farms and chip manufacturers to issue shares in the United States. However, I wouldn't get too thrilled right now because the company is currently losing money. They recorded a 90 million loss last year. A tiny loss in comparison to the money they must generate, but still not ideal for an IPO. Of course, this was back when Bitcoin was nowhere like as interesting as it is now. We also saw a halving last year, which suggests that demand for specialized and optimized Asic mining chips is likely to have increased significantly.

It will be interesting to see what data are eventually revealed if and when that IPO is filed. While all of the buzz surrounding cryptocurrency startup IPOs is fascinating, it raises an essential question. Is it anything you should think about? Of course, it all depends on the pricing, but even then, I would be extremely cautious. This boils down to a single reason. IPOs, especially those as heralded as Coinbase, typically have a long line of wealthy investors waiting to buy those equities. These guys have large accounts and receive first dibs on the offering price. This offering price is almost always lower than the opening price on the first day of business. In the instance of Coinbase, for example, the investment bank advising them on the IPO is none other than Goldman Sachs. You don't believe Goldman has a large list of institutional accounts itching to get their hands on some Coinbase shares? These individuals will then enter at the offer price and acquire their allocation well before the shares are traded on the exchanges. The shopping frenzy on the first day of trade will next be evaluated. If they believe they can make a handsome profit, they will sell them on the open market and watch the stock plummet. It's nearly identical to whales dumping tokens on the crypto market the instant they're listed on an exchange.

By the way, there is a lot of precedent for this in the stock market. It happened on Facebook's first trading day. The same thing happened with Uber, and more recently with Doordash and Airbnb's IPO. In overhyped stocks, the initial day, and even weeks, of trading can be quite tumultuous. You won't get the same bargain that investment bankers provide their buddies at hedge funds and mutual funds. On Wall Street, you're at the bottom of the food chain. This is something that worries me about the Coinbase listing; in particular, many crypto traders will see this as an opportunity to buy a piece of Coinbase. According to the FTX futures market, there is already a large premium on the valuation. However, this IPO is expected to attract more than just your average crypto altcoin gambler. You must also examine the Robin Hood army's impact.

All joking aside, this emerging class of stock speculators has recently been responsible for driving up the prices of a number of corporations. The point I'm trying to make is that when these Coinbase shares hit the market, the buzz will be out of control. Many of these regular investors will buy the shares on the first day, regardless of price, only to see the euphoria fade as bankers and hedge funds line their wallets. However, this does not exclude you from purchasing Coinbase stock. If history is any guide, as the hoopla wears off, fundamental valuation takes over and the price recovers during the bargain-hunting stages. Look no farther than the Facebook IPO, which initially plunged on the first day of trading. It continued to decline for nearly a month, eventually reaching a figure that was 50% less than the initial listing price. Of course, this created an incredible bargain-hunting opportunity for those who saw its genuine long-term potential.

If you had invested in Facebook after the first lows, you would have more than tenfold your money by today. This is something you should keep in mind when the Coinbase listing day arrives. Be aware that the hoopla surrounding that listing will be out of this world. The Fomo will be turned up to 11 as bankers strive to drum up interest in the launch. But as long as you remember what you've read here, you'll be much more prepared to cope with this Fomo when it arrives. To summarize, I am quite pleased about the Coinbase IPO. Not because I want to invest in it, but because of what it represents. It's another proof that crypto isn't just a cypherpunk's fantasy. The days of an obscure exchange called MT Gox dominating a nascent market for this magical internet money are long gone. We will have a crypto exchange playing in the big boys Sandbox of regular equity markets next year, and Coinbase will most likely be the first. A number of other exchanges, mining farms, chip manufacturers, and financing businesses are keeping an eye on the IPO, waiting for their chance to take the market by storm.

However, despite the excitement that these IPOs are likely to generate, they will not be a suitable investment. Not right away, at any rate. You are unlikely to get in at the offer price unless you have a friend who has a line into the Goldman Sachs syndication desk. Don't let the excitement around these IPOs impair your judgment on underlying value. There is wisdom in remaining quiet and waiting to observe how events unfold. Allow other retail investors who haven't done their homework to be the traditional IPO dump guinea pigs. The rational investor has longevity in these times. Of course, institutional investors may be unwilling to deal with a cryptocurrency exchange. That Robin Hood investors would prefer pump insolvent penny stocks than invest in Coinbase or a similar startup. This could give you a good opportunity to buy a stock that you believe is inexpensive, and if you do hold some Coinbase shares, you won't be so hard done by those high trading fees. This is because some of those fees may be repaid in the form of dividends.